CORPORATE

Caffeine

**Boosting B2B Growth
through Sales and Marketing Alignment**

DACIA COFFEY

CORPORATE CAFFEINE
BOOSTING B2B GROWTH THROUGH SALES AND MARKETING ALIGNMENT

Copyright © 2022 Dacia Coffey.

All rights reserved. No part of this book may be used or reproduced by any means, graphic, electronic, or mechanical, including photocopying, recording, taping or by any information storage retrieval system without the written permission of the author except in the case of brief quotations embodied in critical articles and reviews.

Scripture quotations are taken from the Holy Bible, New International Version®. NIV®. Copyright © 1973, 1978, 1984 by International Bible Society. Used by permission of Zondervan. All rights reserved. [Biblica]

iUniverse books may be ordered through booksellers or by contacting:

iUniverse
1663 Liberty Drive
Bloomington, IN 47403
www.iuniverse.com
844-349-9409

Because of the dynamic nature of the Internet, any web addresses or links contained in this book may have changed since publication and may no longer be valid. The views expressed in this work are solely those of the author and do not necessarily reflect the views of the publisher, and the publisher hereby disclaims any responsibility for them.

Any people depicted in stock imagery provided by Getty Images are models, and such images are being used for illustrative purposes only.
Certain stock imagery © Getty Images.

ISBN: 978-1-6632-1926-8 (sc)
ISBN: 978-1-6632-1927-5 (e)

Library of Congress Control Number: 2022900375

Print information available on the last page.

iUniverse rev. date: 07/01/2022

To Kyle.

Thank you from the bottom of my heart for launching me on this journey. You make me brave.

ABOUT THE AUTHOR

A leading authority on accelerating revenue growth, Dacia Coffey is a fractional chief marketing officer and the CEO of The Marketing Blender, an award-winning marketing agency. She has led more than one hundred organizational transformations by helping businesses nail the right message and align sales and marketing efforts to eliminate waste in the business-development process. She is a member of the Forbes Agency Council and a Forbes contributor and was also named an American Advertising Federation Shooting Star. Drawing from her experience as a top-tier sales professional, copywriter, and three-time business owner, Dacia offers high-energy style and surprising insights to deliver both motivation and actionable tips for catalyzing change and growth. In addition to maintaining her client work, she is the host of the *Corporate Caffeine* podcast and writes and speaks on how people can use their work and words to unleash their potential and change the world. Dacia lives in Fort Worth, Texas, with her husband and their four boys. She's a yogi and a runner and geeks out over great conversation, new experiences, and the endless miracles of God's world.

CONTENTS

Preface xi
Introduction xv

Chapter 1   A Business-Development Crossroads 1
Chapter 2   The Payoff of Marketing and Sales Alignment 11
Chapter 3   Buyer Personas 19
Chapter 4   Effective Marketing Plans Made Easy 33
Chapter 5   Messaging 59
Chapter 6   Buying Psychology and Branding 77
Chapter 7   Execution and ROI 101

Encouragement 113
Resources for Your Team 117
Notes 119

PREFACE

Why have I decided to write a book? Because every day in every industry, I watch our busy world and our busyness kill the art of communication. Communication is how you and I understand each other and manage to get our needs met. If you don't communicate well, you simply don't get what you want. As a fractional chief marketing officer, a speaker, and the CEO of a marketing agency, I've worked closely with hundreds of CEOs and business-development teams in the last ten years, and I see communication sabotage as a leading problem—even a leading indicator—in sales plateaus, revenue declines, slim margins, culture breakdowns, and high turnover. Every day, I see a desire to rush through communication in the name of making progress on to-do lists. But what happens when you realize too late that the people around you didn't understand what you said? You have to rewind, rework, and redo. Now extend this repetitive loop of misunderstanding into your business development, where your prospective customers don't understand you. You end up with expensive marketing campaigns, a lack of quality leads, extremely long sales cycles, unreliable projections, missed quotas, client churn, and disillusioned employees. Your organization and your personal work life can and should be better than this.

I wrote this book for the leaders, marketers, and sales professionals in business-to-business, or B2B, industries who want more—more results, more satisfaction, more sanity—and are asking themselves, "Does growth really have to be this hard?" When you harness the power of communication and align it through your marketing and sales (and ideally across your entire organization), the results are spectacular. Great communication is critical to great business success, and I want to give you a system for leveraging communication in your marketing and sales. I've seen firsthand, in small and large companies alike, how a true communication transformation can result in a financial transformation. This approach helped a European manufacturing company turn around a failing US entry strategy. It's helped IT experts get elusive C-suite meetings with the world's largest companies. One executive coach ended a dry spell when we rewrote his sales script, resulting in four ideal clients in less than two months. I've assisted numerous companies in attracting investors and buyers by improving their messages and brands. This approach has even helped HR departments attract and retain top talent by energizing their communications.

The possibility of moving from pain to prosperity is exhilarating not only because success feels good but because there is a lot more at stake than dollars and deals. Work problems don't stay contained within the square footage of people's offices. The people behind these struggles take their frustration home, their stress affects their families, and they begin to disengage from both their work and their joy. Seeing these scenarios firsthand reminds me of the 2006 Adam Sandler movie *Click*.[1] In the movie, Michael (played by Sandler)—a businessman and family man—is impatient for success and generally unsatisfied in his life. He is given a remote control that allows him to fast-forward through the frustrating or boring parts of his life. As he uses the remote, it learns his preferences, and before long, he has gone into autopilot so frequently in his day-to-day life that it's cost him his family, his enjoyment, and eventually his life. Much of what he chooses to skip are the tedious details and mundane conversations, but life happens in those details and conversations. I'm sad to say that I'm watching this metaphor play out in real offices, homes, and Zoom calls more and more frequently, and it must stop. Who we are happens in the cracks and crevices of our waking hours. What we stand for is exemplified in our choices and actions every day, not *someday*. This is just as true at the organizational level as it is at the individual level. When we fast-forward through our communication (personal, team, sales, and marketing), we miss the opportunities we've been waiting for to provide clarity, pique curiosity, build a connection, elicit a response, and show up in our full potential.

Additionally, communication isn't just about our own effectiveness. It can also be a gift we receive when we listen. If you desire to be a student of life, you must be open to the wisdom around you, even if it's not what you want to hear. I share this from experience. When I worked for DeWalt power tools right out of college, I was neck-deep in the frustration many women feel in male-dominated industries. But I was lucky to have managers who were willing to tell me the truth when I tried to emulate the masculine way of communicating, which did *not* work for me. That lesson has made me effective and successful in a dozen male-dominated industries today and has saved me from unhelpful bitterness. When I worked in pharmaceutical sales, I had to learn how to maximize thirty-second interactions with physicians and learned very quickly how to get attention and help people remember my message. When we moved from Atlanta, Georgia, to Corpus Christi, Texas, for my husband's career, I was drowning in isolation and dirty diapers while my husband was on cloud nine in his newfound success and adventure. I had to learn that I was communicating resentment so clearly that I was turning our house into an environment as toxic as a nuclear accident. Two decades later, I still use that lesson to be the best wife, mom, and leader I possibly can be. Each time, I had to learn to look at communication in a new light by slowing down and choosing to understand over being understood. And once I did understand, the key to success and joy was mine.

Now don't get me wrong: I'm still writing a business book, but the truth of the matter is that this communication deterioration is a human condition. Business leaders are human. Employees are human. Customers are human. The communication patterns we develop—or don't develop, because of our fast-forward inclinations—affect everything. There is rarely a real difference between how we communicate in our personal lives and how we communicate in our business lives. It's all personal. In *The Purpose Driven Life*, Rick Warren writes, "Often we act as if relationships are something to be squeezed into our schedule. We talk about *finding* time for our children *or making* time for people in our lives. That gives the impression that relationships are just a part of our lives along with many other tasks. But God says relationships are what life is all about."[2] Think about that. *Nothing* else matters but how you treat people. Countless movies, stories, and personal anecdotes tell us that life's regrets are always and only about lost relationships. Yet we organize our time, attention, and money around tasks, activities, and the acquisition of *things*. "I just have to get this off my list" is the common refrain among adults in all stages and stations of life. Our nature is created for relationships; every business in existence serves other people. If a business doesn't meet a need or desire of other human beings, it *will* go out of business. But many of our businesses are not purposefully in alignment with this idea.

Your communication is a signal of what matters most to you. Owning your communication—heck, simply gaining awareness of your communication—can send off a positive cascade of change in your life and in your business. To own your communication, you need to be intentional in the words, visuals, and processes that tell your story, as well as how you distribute these communications to the market. These intentional choices then need to be given to both your marketing and sales teams so they have the clarity they need to best engage the market.

Your communication is an extension of who you are and what you believe.

People buy from those they know, like, and trust. Is your communication helping people to know, like, and trust you? My experience in both my personal life and my professional life has taught me that great communication is the outward tool that we can use to create profoundly positive changes in our lives, in our businesses, and in the world at large. I hope that as you read this book, it serves you in two ways. First, I want to help business leaders achieve success in a saner and more profitable way by strategically aligning their marketing and sales communications. Second, I hope that you will experience a paradigm shift and harvest lessons that can expand your influence and your whole life. If you choose to act on the advice herein, not only will this book help you stop the waste of marketing dollars, loss of sales opportunities, and the maddening frustration of slow progress, but you will enrich the journey itself for everyone involved.

INTRODUCTION

When you build a better mousetrap, open your door and
beat a path to the world—a path made of words.
—Sims Wyeth[3]

It has never been more difficult for companies to clearly and effectively communicate their value than it is in today's world. Marketing tools, tactics, and channels can target almost anyone, anywhere, at any time, and as each year passes, the convergence of new technologies adds more choice, nuance, and complexity to our marketing options. And with the increasing speed of change comes less time to get it right. Campaigns and marketing messages are so prolific in our day-to-day lives that they don't have the impact and power to influence us like they once did. Our marketers have less and less time to keep pace with how to adjust the messaging and imagery to maximize the effectiveness of these campaigns. The less resonant and bland the message, the more our market tunes it out and the less return on investment (ROI) we get from our spend. Additionally, the challenge of attributing a specific sale to a specific marketing tactic is nearly impossible, creating massive friction between leadership and marketing teams. In business-to-business, or B2B, industries with complex and often technical messaging, where marketing creates influence for sales teams to close the deal, the struggle to develop and evolve a powerful and aligned message that moves the market is magnified exponentially.

Meanwhile, for all its challenges, modern marketing has effectively and permanently changed the face of the sales landscape because now decision makers have easy and immediate access to the information they need to research different solutions, ideas, and providers. Salespeople get less in-person time with prospects, must send more follow-ups, and are often blind to how their prospects have changed their points of view as the buying process has progressed. Who knows what blogs, videos, or reviews they've digested and how those things have changed their buying criteria? And since the pandemic, sales teams now must learn to be effective in social selling and the use of video technology to build trust and relationships.

Making matters worse, sales and marketing have drifted into separate divisions in formal and informal organizational charts, creating a chasm of strategic gaps and misalignment that swallow opportunity and effectiveness.

But it doesn't have to be like this. In this book, I'm going to walk you through how to implement an aligned strategy across your total business-development system so you can grow faster and get better ROI. I'll show you how to choose and distribute words, visuals, and experiences to resonate with your prospects and customers at a gut level, sparking inquiry, desire, and action in your day-to-day marketing execution. What I intend to give you is an understanding of how and why your marketing will work, as well as a system to prevent the busyness of modern life from distracting you from maximum impact. Leaders want more growth and ROI. Salespeople want commission. Marketers want more recognition for their impact on the business. If we look closely, we see everyone wants the same thing—growth—but we refer to our common goals with very different words, derailing progress and unity. I wrote this book for the B2B leader, salesperson, and marketer because they all deserve—and their organizations need—a playbook for how to align messaging and the business-development strategy to drive outstanding outcomes.

If you'll indulge me, I'm going to ask a stupid question. It's one that I believe will change your results. But it's also a question that could cause you to roll your eyes and throw this book in the trash. I'm willing to take the risk, and I think you should play along. So here it is: "What is marketing?"

The word *marketing* has come to mean many different things in today's world. There are so many approaches and tactics to choose from. But what I'm seeing with my clients and in the industry at large is that the semantics behind the word *marketing* can do one of two things: (1) it can act as a key to unlock a powerful strategy for aligning marketing with the rest of the business (especially sales), or (2) it can derail the company's success under the guise of busyness, "visibility," and meaningless key performance indicators.

The broad definition taught in college is that marketing encompasses all the processes involved in getting a product or service from the manufacturer or seller to the ultimate consumer. This is typically divided into the four (or sometimes five) Ps: product, price, promotion, and place (and sometimes people).[4] This definition is expansive considering how entangled this becomes with operations. The first definition in *Merriam-Webster*, broken into two parts, seems easier to digest, with the focus on promotion and selling: "the act or process of selling or purchasing in a market; the process or technique of promoting, selling, and distributing a product or service."[5] It's a bit too trite for my taste. The American Marketing Association defines *marketing* as "the activity, set of institutions, and processes for creating, communicating, delivering, and exchanging offerings that have value for customers, clients, partners, and society at large."[6] This is where it gets interesting. Because, for business-to-consumer, or B2C, products, the original provider of the product or service isn't there in person to convince you what to buy. Preplanned messages, promotions, and tactics must do all the convincing for you.

Not so with B2B. If you look at any of these definitions, the sales function is rolled up into marketing. But rarely do org charts reflect this definition. More often than not, the marketing department is doing their thing (i.e., the preplanned messages, promotions, and tactics so critical to B2C success), but with minimal confirmation of their direct impact on sales. Meanwhile, the sales team is working to move deals forward without understanding what has influenced the buyers' current perspectives, thus lacking the benefit of the big-picture thinking that could speed up sales cycles and even increase the scope of the deals they are chasing.

So what's *my* definition of *marketing*? It is to evoke desire in a specific audience and remove the fear of loss, which will lead to a sale. With this definition, you are forced to put the customer first. "To evoke desire" has everything to do with *why* individuals buy and nothing to do with what they buy. And therein lies the magic of truly effective marketing: a purchasing decision is always a means to an end, *not* an end in itself.

- o People buy luxury cars because of how those acquisitions make them feel and how they want to be perceived.
- o Parents buy their children expensive sports equipment because they want to help their children be successful in any way possible.
- o Contractors buy new equipment because it will help them land bigger jobs.
- o Business owners buy enterprise resource planning software to make their teams more efficient and to remove the guesswork in the data.

What Do People Really Want?

In business, we may want to

wield more influence,
grow sales,
grow profits,
be well known,
impress others,
have more freedom,
feel confident,
get rid of doubt and fear,
feel happy,
be liked,
feel loved,
be recognized,
be in control,
take a break, or
be capable.

Our professional motivators might be

likability,
power,
success,
influence,
money,
time,
peace,
love,
fulfillment, or
freedom.

We are in the business of tapping into what people *actually* want and who they want to be.

In my work as a chief marketing officer (CMO), almost every time I'm introduced to a marketing or sales team, I find that the everyday business-development communication is being treated as a checklist:

- ✓ Send the follow-up email.
- ✓ Update the contact in the CRM.
- ✓ Tweak last week's proposal for the next prospect.
- ✓ Create a new brochure for the new product launch.
- ✓ Write the month's social media posts.
- ✓ Update three slides in the PowerPoint presentation for Wednesday's pitch.
- ✓ Write the blurb for the next webinar topic.
- ✓ Tell the team to do a new company video.
- ✓ Follow up with three prospects.

I recognize that people are trying to organize their productivity, but your marketing and sales communications sell for you when you're not in the room. (With 2020 in our rearview mirror, we cannot forget how critical this is!) These emails, social media posts, blogs, videos, ads, brochures, and the like communicate your value, integrity, and ability to help people achieve their goals.

Where in this list is the intention to serve others, solve problems, bring value, or stand out? Your prospective customer is on a path to solve a problem. Your team is progressing one deal at a time to a total sales goal. Your marketing and business communication is supposed to provide tools to guide both parties on their shared pilgrimage. But customers and companies alike are getting lost along the way. In our busyness, we easily forget to fulfill our promise to help others get what they want when we're engaged in communication.

Sales and marketing are often disparaged as manipulative or insincere, but if done right, a great business-development approach puts servant leadership at the heart of your communication. Servant leadership places the needs of those you serve at the heart of your efforts. So if your business exists to meet a need or fill a desire, doesn't it make sense that the way you communicate, market, and sell should facilitate your best outcome? Spoiler alert: a servant-leadership approach often garners better results.

> Did you know that most B2B sales end in a so-called no-decision decision? This means that the prospects know they have a problem and spend a large amount of their time researching and interviewing companies to help them and then never make a single bit of progress on the thing causing them trouble.

It's my intention to help you bring this servant-leadership philosophy into direct orchestration with your sales and marketing to produce excellent results for your customers and your revenue growth. As you progress through this book, you'll see that I've organized the chapters around central strategic themes. At the end of each chapter, I provide a bullet-pointed "Rearview Mirror" summary to help you retain the key takeaways, with each chapter acting like teeth in a wheel, meshing to create a growth engine for your company. I've also created additional resources and worksheets that you can download from DaciaCoffey.com to help you execute these ideas. I believe that when you apply servant-leadership principles and unify your business-development communication under this philosophy, you will not only unleash your organizational-growth potential but, through your work, maximize the individual impact you were meant to have in this world. You can use this book to create meaning, connection, and prosperity for all. Grab your coffee and your sense of possibility, and let's dive in.

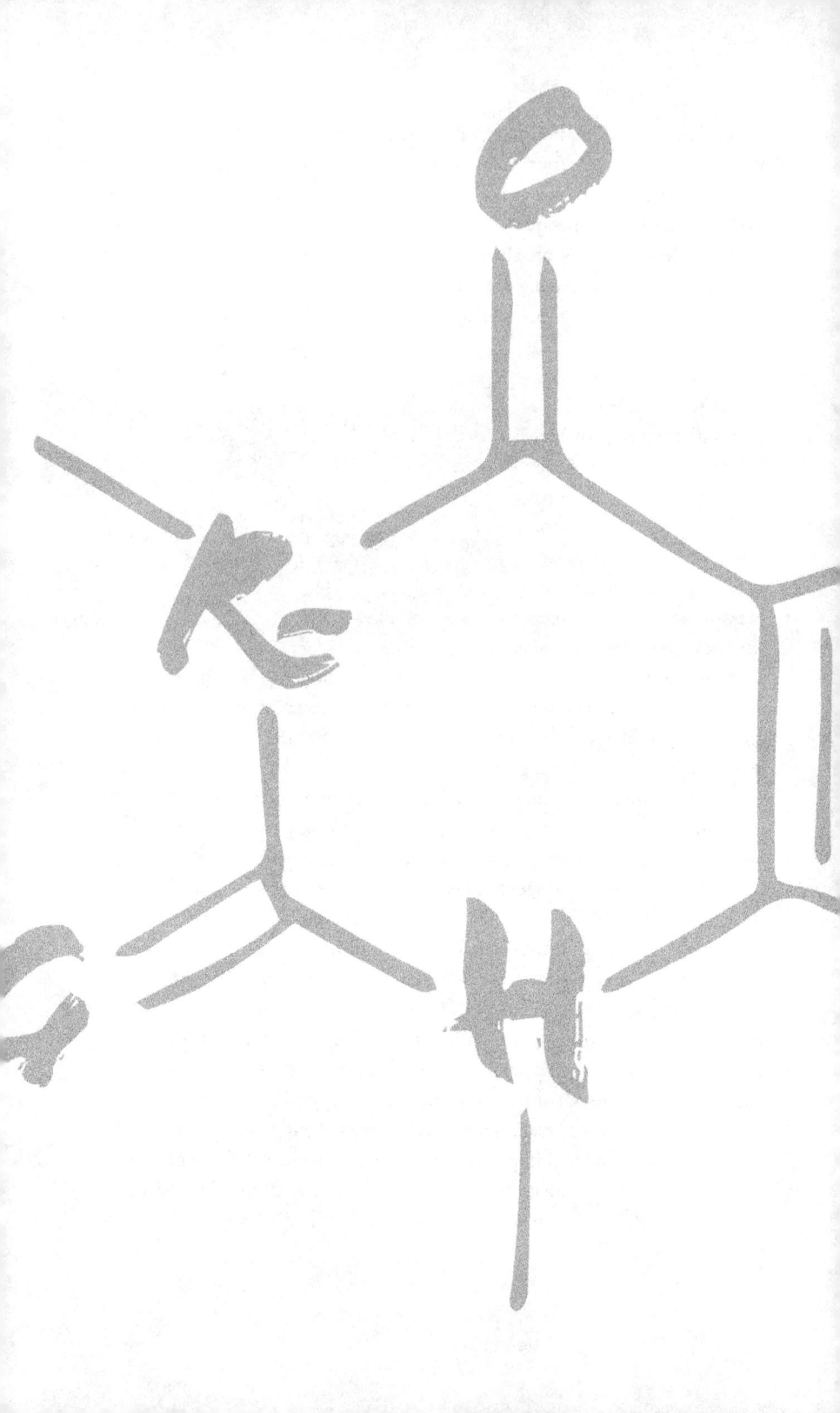

A BUSINESS-DEVELOPMENT CROSSROADS

The traditional consultative selling approach is no longer scalable. With the buyers in control of the research and vendor-selection phase of the sales cycle, marketing is how you get your name and your message in front of the right people at the right time. However, sales and marketing misalignment can cost companies opportunity and profit. The key is to create a holistic business-development system grounded in the humanity behind the sale.

In 1861, John Wanamaker, the son of a brickmaker, founded the first department store in Philadelphia. He had a reputation for honesty and was a merchandising genius. His stores were grand, featuring ostentatious architectural elements that acted as the bold backdrop for lavish events, concerts, and light shows—all to attract a crowd, in hopes that, once there, they would shop. Wanamaker is widely acknowledged as one of the fathers of modern advertising. Yet at a speech in front of the Merchants' Association, he famously said, "Half the money I spend on advertising is wasted; the trouble is I don't know which half."[7]

Most people repeat his quotation to denigrate the effectiveness of marketing, but that's not actually what Wanamaker was getting at. He was in New York for the association meeting, and the title of his talk was "Advertising as a Business Force." From his podium, he challenged the audience by pointing out that he didn't believe advertisers gave enough serious thought to how and why their ads would work. He gave his speech before the internet, before TV, before mobile devices and apps, and before globalization. His point was intensely valid then, and its truth remains unchallenged today. Do you know how and why your marketing will work?

Marketing is both an art and a science. It doesn't have a finish line, yet in the business-to-business, or B2B, world, it is often treated as something to check off the list. Worse, as soon as a certain type of tactic evolves to maximum effectiveness, everyone jumps on it, and it's time for a new revolution to cut through the sea of sameness. And it's always been this way.

By the end of this book, you should know how and why your marketing will work.

That's what Wanamaker wanted for his fellow businesspeople, and this is what I want for you. You need a way to take your marketing dollars more seriously and put them to work for the good of your organization and the good of the world. We can look at your operations as the engine that powers your business, and your sales and marketing efforts as the fuel that drives your business forward. You can go for a short while on the gas you have in the tank, but eventually, you'll run out. You must fuel your organization with quality opportunities. Marketing is that fuel.

But, you might argue, Wanamaker sold consumer goods; what about the more complicated exchanges of business products and services, where the decisions are about not just wants and needs but the health and effectiveness of whole organizations and groups of people? You must close business belly to belly in this environment—what's marketing got to do with that?

A BUSINESS-DEVELOPMENT CROSSROADS

The traditional consultative selling approach is no longer scalable. With the buyers in control of the research and vendor-selection phase of the sales cycle, marketing is how you get your name and your message in front of the right people at the right time. However, sales and marketing misalignment can cost companies opportunity and profit. The key is to create a holistic business-development system grounded in the humanity behind the sale.

In 1861, John Wanamaker, the son of a brickmaker, founded the first department store in Philadelphia. He had a reputation for honesty and was a merchandising genius. His stores were grand, featuring ostentatious architectural elements that acted as the bold backdrop for lavish events, concerts, and light shows—all to attract a crowd, in hopes that, once there, they would shop. Wanamaker is widely acknowledged as one of the fathers of modern advertising. Yet at a speech in front of the Merchants' Association, he famously said, "Half the money I spend on advertising is wasted; the trouble is I don't know which half."[7]

Most people repeat his quotation to denigrate the effectiveness of marketing, but that's not actually what Wanamaker was getting at. He was in New York for the association meeting, and the title of his talk was "Advertising as a Business Force." From his podium, he challenged the audience by pointing out that he didn't believe advertisers gave enough serious thought to how and why their ads would work. He gave his speech before the internet, before TV, before mobile devices and apps, and before globalization. His point was intensely valid then, and its truth remains unchallenged today. Do you know how and why your marketing will work?

Marketing is both an art and a science. It doesn't have a finish line, yet in the business-to-business, or B2B, world, it is often treated as something to check off the list. Worse, as soon as a certain type of tactic evolves to maximum effectiveness, everyone jumps on it, and it's time for a new revolution to cut through the sea of sameness. And it's always been this way.

By the end of this book, you should know how and why your marketing will work.

That's what Wanamaker wanted for his fellow businesspeople, and this is what I want for you. You need a way to take your marketing dollars more seriously and put them to work for the good of your organization and the good of the world. We can look at your operations as the engine that powers your business, and your sales and marketing efforts as the fuel that drives your business forward. You can go for a short while on the gas you have in the tank, but eventually, you'll run out. You must fuel your organization with quality opportunities. Marketing is that fuel.

But, you might argue, Wanamaker sold consumer goods; what about the more complicated exchanges of business products and services, where the decisions are about not just wants and needs but the health and effectiveness of whole organizations and groups of people? You must close business belly to belly in this environment—what's marketing got to do with that?

Everything. I argue that most B2B companies opt to drive sedans in a Formula 1 race when they choose to place marketing in a silo apart from the "real" business. The acceleration of technology and the proliferation of marketing approaches have wreaked havoc on the traditional consultative selling because today's buyers bounce among referral information, online research, and information in the sales cycle to form a singular opinion about the worthiness of a product or service offering. Here's a startling statistic: 2011 to 2017 resulted in seven years of declining sales-quota attainment among B2B sellers. The percentage of salespeople who hit their quota finally leveled off in 2018 at a pitiful 54 percent.[9] Let me repeat that: less than 60 percent make quota! Why is this happening, and why isn't this more widely discussed?

Traditional sales models are simply no longer scalable, because they function on a one-to-one level: one salesperson making one call at a time, having one meeting at a time, to land one deal at a time. But on average, there are eight decision makers in the average B2B sale.[10] Each of one them will need to be moved forward in the sales cycle, but B2B buyers are pushing sales reps farther out of the sales cycle. Let's look at the following numbers:

- B2B buyers say they are 57 percent of the way through their decision before they even meet a sales rep.[11]
- Ninety-four percent of business buyers do online research.[12]
- B2B buyers engage with thirteen pieces of content before deciding on a vendor.[13]

"Value of Advertising," New York *Daily Tribune*, March 17, 1898:

Robert C. Ogden, the resident partner of the firm of John Wanamaker, delivered a forceful and convincing address yesterday at the second meeting of the convention of the Merchants' Association of New-York, on "Advertising as a Business Force." …

> Another experience that goes largely in ordinary advertising is the waste of money. There have been many calculations concerning the vast sums of money expended upon advertising in this country. I do not recall what their magnitude is, but the figures compiled by intelligent observers are really astounding. I think if we could manage to analyze that expenditure of money we would find that a vast percentage of it, probably one-half, is entirely wasted. One reason for this waste is that the advertiser does not regard his advertising with sufficient seriousness. If he would take it more seriously, he would study its principles and its methods, and would save a great deal of money.[8]

Buyers are engaging with sellers later and later in the process because they can now research and frame their decisions on their own via the internet. Buyers now control the research portion of the sales cycle. Thus, your brand recognition, digital marketing, and content (i.e., your marketing) will be what earn you a seat at the table. However, even for those who have brand recognition, digital marketing, and content, it's never been more difficult to be memorable and unique and to be heard, desired, and trusted. Research shows that you have only a few seconds to get someone's attention. Every day, a person comes in contact with roughly 5,000 brands and more than 350 ads and receives 121 emails and 94 texts. Your marketing had better be good enough to compete with all of that.

This highly competitive landscape is part of a world overrun with distractions. In this always-on world, all aspects of a person's life can leak into any given scenario at any time. While researching your offering and your competitor's, your decision maker could be doing any of the following, for example:

- ✓ eating lunch
- ✓ arguing with his wife via text
- ✓ getting an email for a hiring request
- ✓ stressing out knowing he has to fire an employee at the end of the day
- ✓ deciding what to do about this year's family vacation
- ✓ preparing to calm an angry client
- ✓ nursing a hangover
- ✓ negotiating a deal
- ✓ crunching numbers

The list goes on. And as if that weren't overwhelming enough, millennials and those of Generation Z have grown up completely submerged in the noise; unsurprisingly, they yield a high level of skepticism toward salespeople and marketing messages at large. This is the face of the B2B new decision maker.

And now, in a postpandemic world, we have less travel, less face-to-face time, Zoom fatigue, social selling, and automation, as well as artificial intelligence both speeding up interruptions and blocking interruptions.

It is no longer feasible for a salesperson to manage the full spectrum of the sales cycle, from prospecting, or generating leads; to negotiating and closing a deal; to maintaining a relationship to cross-sell and upsell future contracts. It's simply not the highest and best use of a talented salesperson's time. Just the sheer number of follow-ups it takes to maintain contact is astounding—and higher than it's ever been.

Many sales reps struggle to make it past three follow-up contacts; it takes a lot of discipline to follow up five or more times and even more discipline to bring increasing value and individualization to the budding relationship.

So many leaders I speak to lament that it's nearly impossible to find great sales talent anymore. But I'd argue this is false. You're simply asking a single person to keep up with or compete with the mass production of business communication. According to a 2018 CSO Insights study, the top 20 percent of salespeople account for more than 50 percent of an organization's revenues.[14] This creates a double jeopardy, because what happens when your top performers are poached by your competition? You must have a strategy and processes in place that do not rely solely on superstar salespeople. Superstars are not scalable, but strategy and processes are.

Simply put, it's incredibly difficult to be successful in today's B2B sales environment. And it's made all the more difficult because most B2B marketing is dull and wordy and does little to build a bridge that will bring together the people who will collaborate one day to solve an organizational problem. Business-to-consumer, or B2C, marketing is not intrinsically interesting. There is nothing inherently fascinating about insurance, body spray, or fried bits of flour coated in cheese dust. What is interesting is how the marketing aligns with how we see the world. We can and should do this in B2B.

We are past due for a widespread movement toward aligning sales

You are competing against *all* of this:

average attention span	8.25 seconds
average commute	52 minutes round trip
time spent in meetings	50%
average number of emails per day	121
hours in front of a screen der day	12
words read on average website page	28%
brands per day	5,000+
ads per day	362
touches to get a lead	7–13
salespeople who will miss quota	54%

and marketing, and thus, there is no current agreement on how to do this. While the acceleration of technology, sales, and marketing has given us an amazing body of knowledge and tools to communicate, it's also left us with very little time to incorporate and customize these best practices to our individual environments. This has led to increased buyer frustration and disengagement from the marketing message.

The only real way to align marketing and sales *and* be agile enough to evolve your best practices and execution is to adopt a truly customer-centric approach. This means putting a focus on the customer *before* you issue an invoice. This requires a business-development philosophy where the team aligns around a heart of service and meets people's needs from a place of wholeness. It requires an approach where technology and marketing elevate the role of salesperson and create efficiency and confidence for the decision makers.

Why do sales and marketing need to be aligned? Because not only does such an alignment give a more cohesive, higher-value experience to a prospect, but misalignment is wreaking havoc on revenue growth and creating ridiculous amounts of waste in time, leads, money, and opportunity. How dangerous is this misalignment? Some studies show that failure to align sales and marketing teams around the right processes and technologies costs B2B companies 10 percent or more of revenue per year. Additionally, viewing the sales function only through the lens of a sales cycle, instead of a buyer's journey, keeps you at a disadvantage. It is marketing that closes the gap between the two and engages a buyer in the prioritization and research phase. Marketing can provoke action, reframe the decision process, position your offering positively, and get you in the door to access opportunities your salespeople would not be able to find.

But the chasm represents more than an impact on your revenue and financial performance. This misalignment is based on the fact that your sales and marketing teams do not understand each other and are thus unable to work as a unified team. In nearly all the workshops I facilitate, the marketing leaders will tell me later that the workshop was the first time they got the information they needed from the sales team about the market. The missing information—buyer insights, lead qualification, and sales conversations—prevented the marketing team from crafting messages and outreach that would truly bring value and align with the people they're called to reach.

There is no strategy on the planet that can guide an organization to its growth potential if the people within cannot communicate and collaborate effectively. Because of vast access to information, the buyers are in control (or out of control, if you prefer), and you need a unified business-development strategy that serves the buyers where they are and even guides and coaches them through complicated decisions.

These figures are just samplings of the problem, but what's the potential upside? In my experience, it's a significantly lower cost per customer acquisition; a higher level of employee engagement; a lower churn in your business-development teams; and a swift, highly efficient way to break out of sales ruts. But don't just take my word for it. Here are a few studies:

- Sales and marketing alignment can lead to a 32 percent increase in year-over-year revenue growth.[15]
- Sales and marketing alignment can lead to 208 percent growth in marketing revenue.[16]
- Sales and marketing alignment can lead to 38 percent higher sales win rates.[17]
- Sales and marketing alignment can improve sales efforts at closing deals by 67 percent and help marketing teams generate 209 percent more value from their efforts.[18]

And now that we are in a postpandemic world, this is going to be even more critical. With more people working from their at-home desks, we need agreement about what prospect engagement actually looks like.

Sales and marketing alignment is a holistic strategy—a commitment to bringing value to customers at every single engagement *even before they buy from you*. There is no finish line. You must shift your paradigm to value delivery across the full business-development spectrum.

What is the exact nature of this paradigm shift? Well, let's first explore the current approach: you are solving the wrong problem. You're wondering how to better amplify your message, increase your visibility, convince the market that you're better than the competition, and get more meetings—but these are symptoms of the problem, not the real problem. The real problem is that your growth is not about you. Your potential, as an individual and an organization, is based solely on your ability to create a positive transformation for someone else. Your potential is tied to the success you bring to *other people*. The problem you need to solve lies in the question, How do you align your entire organization around the humans you serve? In other words, how do you ensure that all your output brings value to others?

The COVID-19 stay-at-home orders accelerated the digital transformation. Those who learn to optimize their message and their digital tools will reap the rewards. Digital engagement cannot happen without *human engagement*.

With the increase in noise and complexity, only tailored messages will break through; this means you need insightful and targeted messages that have been lovingly crafted for niche groups of people.

Let's start untangling the spaghetti to understand all the options and methodologies available to us and map out a path forward for our own organizations.

The Rearview Mirror

- You need clarity regarding how and why your marketing will be effective.
- The traditional sales model is no longer scalable without the support of marketing.
- The acceleration of technology and the proliferation of marketing approaches have wreaked havoc on traditional consultative selling.
- It's time for a widespread movement in the B2B world to align sales and marketing, and it must occur through the adoption of a truly customer-centric approach that begins before the first invoice is issued.

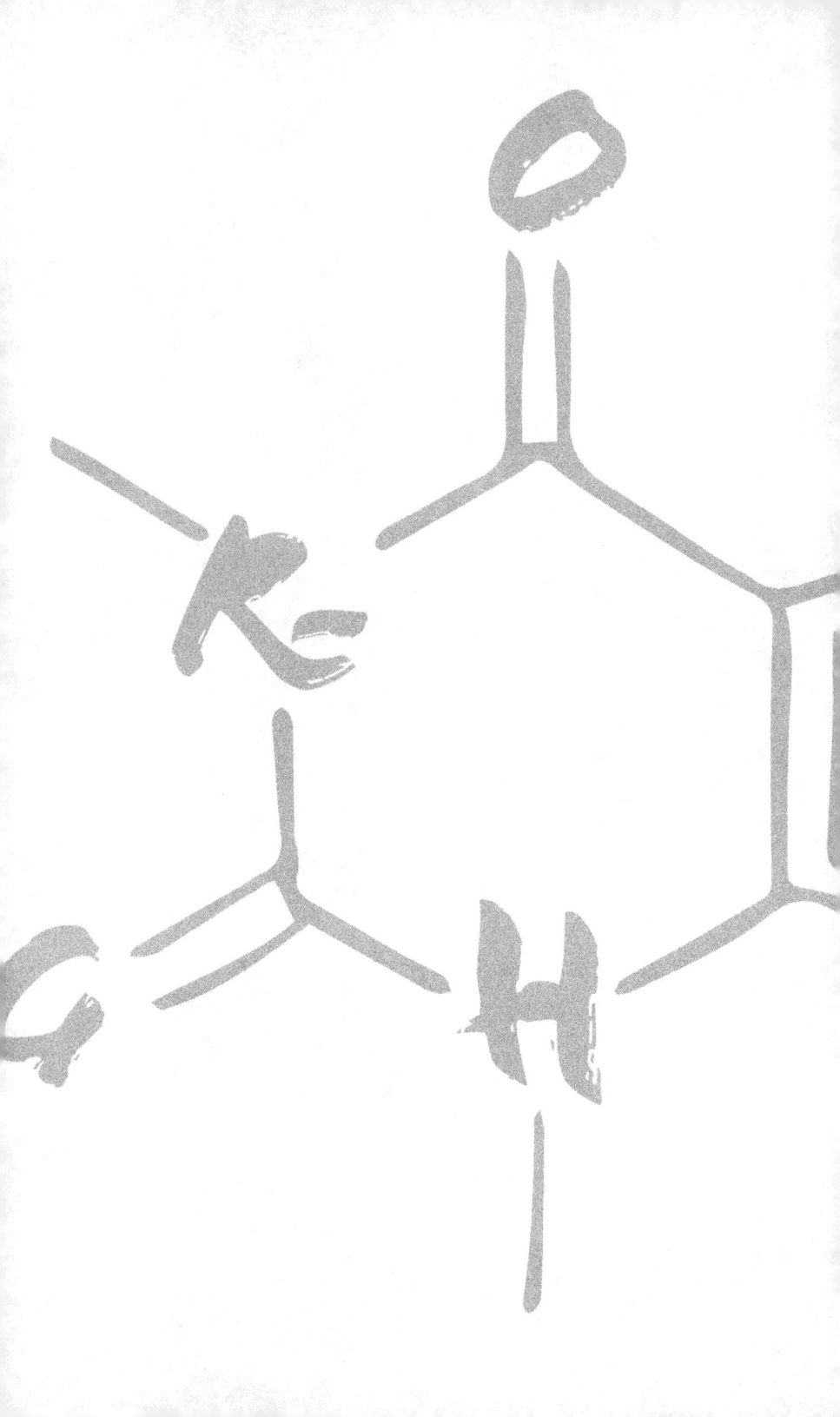

THE PAYOFF OF MARKETING AND SALES ALIGNMENT

While it's reasonable to wonder when your marketing will create measurable results, you should never wonder whether your marketing will work. There are specific strategic elements that must be in place to drive desirable and predictable results. Without them, you will waste money and opportunity.

I have a huge pet peeve that I'm going to share with you, and it shows up in the form of a question: "Will this work?"

"Will this campaign work?"

"Will this message work?"

"Will this idea [event, email, etc.] work?"

This question is the tip of the iceberg that can sink your growth. This question should *never* be tolerated if you are serious about achieving and accelerating growth. It's intolerable because it implies that

1. a single tool or idea can
2. independently and massively drive results in a
3. finite amount of time.

It also might suggest a lack of rationale behind why the tactic or message was chosen. Marketing—business development—is a journey, not a drag race. It's not a race, because races come to an end. Just like you will never get to the point in your life where you no longer have to eat because you've already eaten enough, you'll never get to the point where you can stop marketing because you've already driven enough opportunities your way. The question instead should be "When will we see how well this is working?"

Every business has a vision of long-term success, so why is it so hard to commit to the consistent strategy that will get you there?

> Let us not become weary in doing good, for at the proper time we will reap a harvest if we do not give up.
> —Galatians 6:9

Too often, I see people focus on the tactics and then wonder why the tactics aren't working. The answer is always the lack of strategy or a broken strategic component. And I think I understand why. When you're talking about business development and revenue growth, planning and thinking don't *feel* like progress. However, strategy is the difference between running on a treadmill and running on pavement. If the point is just to run marketing campaigns and put stuff out there, then tactics are good enough. But if the point is to move closer to a major goal or milestone and make real progress, you have to pick a path and run the path one step at a time—that's the strategy part.

Strategy Breeds Consistency

Consistency is the silver bullet. Consistency is what greases the wheel. Consistency is what's missing from many companies' business-development approaches. Everyone wants to hire the superstar salesperson, crack the viral post, launch a culture-changing ad, or make a jaw-dropping impact at an event, but even these actions must be repeated over and over again. I'm always surprised to encounter people's frustration over the fact that marketing costs money. Everyone thinks or hopes that if you build a better mousetrap, the world will beat a path to your door, but it won't. (Ask Apple how well that went before it launched the infamous "1984" commercial. Fast-forward to today: the company doesn't have the best product, but it does have the best marketing—and that has made all the difference.)

If marketing were temporary, short-term, or free, you would actually miss out on the full opportunity your marketing provides. Words create reality. When you fully step into the real potential of marketing and cultivate a message with a servant-leadership heart, you step into the fullness of your influence in the world. Sure, selling a lot is great, but selling a lot and taking a part in a business world full of meaning, connection, and prosperity for all is better—much better.

How to Stop Wasting Money

There are really only two reasons that clients ever hire me to help them with their marketing: (1) to end the frustration of not growing revenue as fast as they should be and (2) to stop the feeling that they are wasting their marketing money on ineffective tactics. The only thing that solves either of these issues is strategy. Conversely, these issues cannot be resolved without a solid strategy. Why? Because at the heart of it, strategy is how we manage uncertainty. And effective communication is the key to implementing and sustaining your business-development strategy.

We've been taught to see strategy as a plan designed to achieve an overarching goal. This is true, of course. For instance, I like this definition of *strategy*: "the art and science of planning and marshaling resources for their most efficient and effective use to bring about a desired future or solution to a problem."[19] But strategy is not a set-it-and-forget-it lever we can pull for business growth. It's the guiding principle we follow to achieve our goals and determine how to handle setbacks and surprises quickly. Strategy creates decision-making criteria. Strategy creates traction. Strategy ensures everyone is headed in the same direction and speaking the same language. Best of all, strategy does not require that everything go right in order for us to achieve success. No one has a crystal ball. Our courses of action always have unknowns—not to mention we all have a tendency to resist change and stay in our comfort zones, which can slow down progress. The danger lies in our failure to acknowledge the unknowns, or when we choose tactics without rationale and without recognition of the basic assumptions we are making about the market.

Your marketing strategy compiles your decision-making criteria for all to see so you can ask the right questions about how to adjust when things don't go as planned. This is important because often companies confuse strategy with tactics and plans. Your strategy is not your plan. Your marketing plan is your plan. Your strategy is the framework that guides the development of your plan and its evolution or improvement. Tactics are the individual elements of your plan, whereas strategy is a big-picture view of how it all comes together. Some business strategists identify the purpose of strategy as attaining a sustainable and competitive edge over the competition, and I think this helps us clarify what strategy is and why it is critical.

Carl von Clausewitz, a Prussian general and military strategist who fought during the Napoleonic Wars, outlined six basic principles of strategic effectiveness, which I think can give excellent insight into understanding strategy through a marketing perspective. His principles were as follows:

1. Advantage of terrain
2. Surprise
3. Attack from several sides
4. Aid to theater of war by means of fortifications
5. Assistance of the people
6. Use of great moral forces

If we extrapolate these principles and apply them to marketing, the elements of strategic effectiveness are as follows:

1. Understanding the market and developing an advantageous position
2. Attracting attention
3. Developing multiple ways to get your message out there

4. Protecting against attack (disruption, commoditization, economic impact, etc.) with innovation and market intelligence
5. Building loyalty and referral strategies internally and externally
6. Knowing what you stand for, communicating it clearly, and helping your team to align around these values

Addressing these strategic elements will help you build and fortify your competitive advantage, and it will help you make maximum usage of your resources. In short, you'll stop wasting your money.

You can look at your strategy as your map. As you decide who will want your offering, how you can reach them, what will convince them to act, and how many of your resources you will marshal to do so, you need to set these details as decision-making landmarks that guide your way. You'll build your map as you progress through this book by creating strategic landmarks to guide your team and your progress. You'll answer the following questions:

1. Who are your ideal buyers? What are their psychographic profiles that help you identify them clearly? Once you know, you steer definitively toward them.
2. What do your ideal buyers care about, and what message will resonate with them?
3. Where do your ideal buyers go for information, and what process do they use to make decisions?
4. What is your actual sales cycle? This helps you visualize the actual patterns of interaction you have with prospects and what role marketing should play. You need to predetermine how marketing should align and support your human relationships and efforts in the real world.
5. What do you stand for?
6. What are you trying to achieve?
7. You need to be clear about your brand and how it communicates not only your value but your values. Does your brand accurately convey the truth of your organization—the truth about who you are and how you act as a group of individuals unified around a common goal or purpose? Is your view of this truth consistent with how you're perceived? This landmark helps your ideal buyers recognize that they are on the right path to solving their problems.

8. How is your offering different from those of your competitors? You need to understand the position you hold in the market and thus the position you hold in the minds of your prospects.

Anytime you read about the history of strategy, it's described as a blend of wisdom, science, craft, and art. I'm not going to lie; marketing is not easy. Marketing takes on the complexity of the human psyche, which can create a powerful long-term advantage. So let's map out your strategy.

The Rearview Mirror

- To stop wasting money and start growing revenue faster, you must shift from a tactical approach to a strategic approach.
- Strategy breeds consistency, and consistency breeds growth.
- When planning, review the six elements of strategic effectiveness in marketing.
- Build strategic landmarks to guide the execution of your business-development plans and revenue growth.

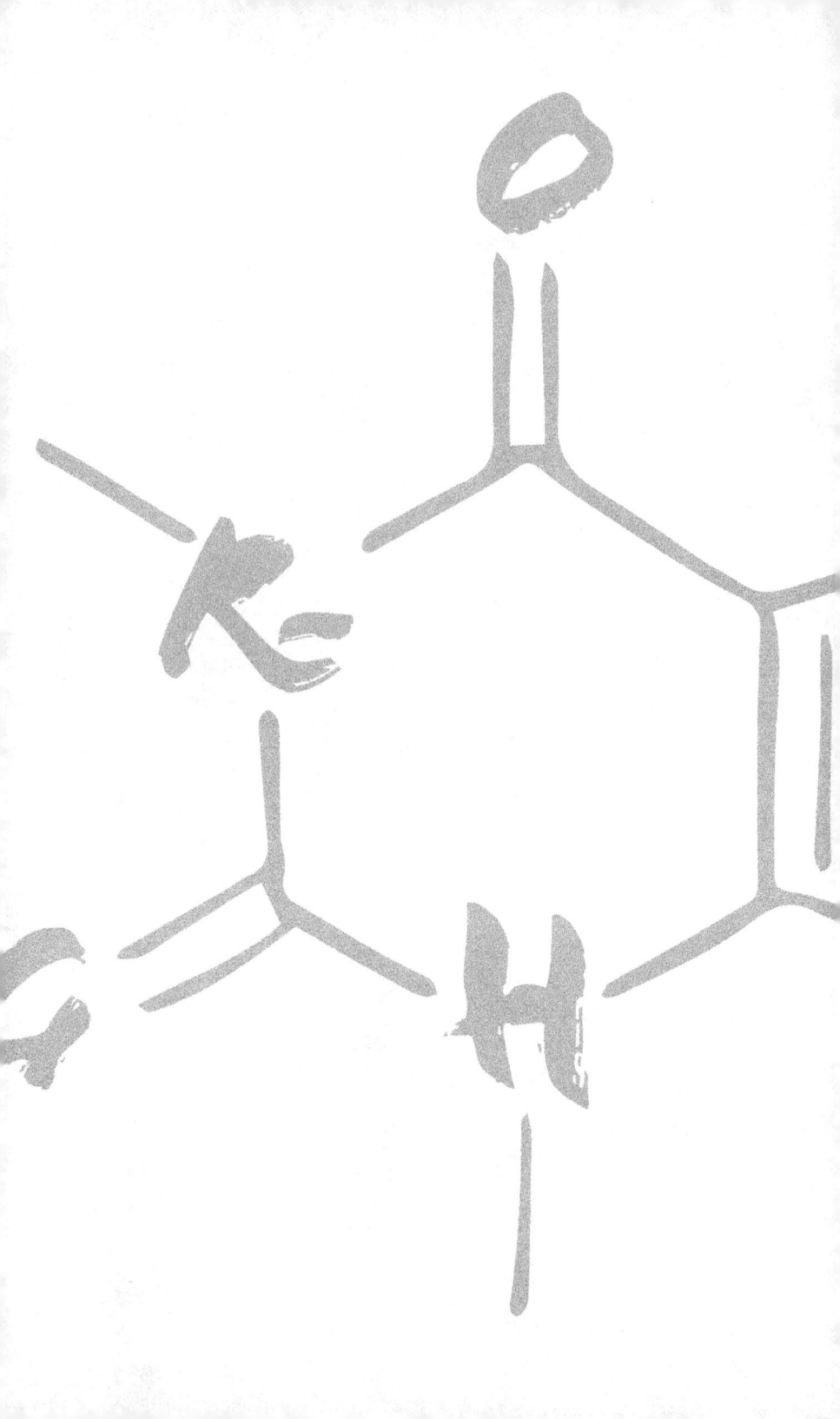

3
BUYER PERSONAS

There is one single unbreakable key to marketing success: you must know your ideal customers intimately. This knowledge, scaled across your organization, will help you develop the right message and the right tactics and can often lead to innovation in your product development. Documenting buyer-persona profiles can create clear decision-making criteria for your total business-development system.

If you get nothing else from this book, if you read just one chapter, let it be this one. This is the make or break of it all: your brand, your message, where and how you advertise, how people find out about you, how you get them to pick you, how you get a meeting, how you close a deal—whether or not you can get and keep customers for the long haul. All of it. This is the whole enchilada. It's so foundational that, at some point in time, even the most disciplined among us will take this for granted because the curse of knowledge takes us further away from the buyer's point of view. We forget what questions we used to have before we developed expertise. We overcomplicate our explanations. Even more dangerously, we begin to solve the wrong problem. We ask, "How can I increase my visibility?" "How can I get my message out?" "How can I stand out from the competition?" and "How can I increase sales?" But these questions lead us to solve the wrong problem.

We cannot be customer centric in our actions and operations if we are self-centered in our problem-solving. As individuals, we all naturally consider our own challenges, goals, and emotions before we extend our concern to others. This might happen in an instant, or it might cloud our judgment for an extended period, but all of us are anchored to our own thoughts and points of view. We are in our own heads. It's a universal human tendency to be centered around our own concerns. But this tendency is the Achilles' heel of many failed efforts.

Your business, your success, your potential is *not about you*. Your revenue and profit come from your ability to deliver a positive transformation in the lives of other people. It's not about you. Period.

If you want people to pick you, to reward you for being excellent at solving their problems, then you need to know them and their problems as intimately as you know your own. And then you need to build every bit of your marketing and sales strategy around what those people care about.

B2B work is not building to building. B2B is still about people. Sure, our products or services help on a divisional or organizational level, but we're still talking about solutions for groups of *people*. I sometimes half-jokingly say that *B2B* actually stands for *belly to belly* because our sales and offerings often require people facing each other, looking each other in the eye. It's intimate, it's personal, and we put our own names on the line as we speak for everyone else at our companies. At the end of the day, it's about two decision makers—community representatives, if you will—deciding to work together.

So the big question this book seeks to answer for you is, What does it take to get to this belly-to-belly meeting and agreement?

Whether it's software, HR solutions, recruiting, raw materials, material-handling products, professional services (legal, marketing, accounting, consulting, etc.), equipment sales, logistics, travel services, or products to be sold through a sales force or stores, all of it—every offering—helps people, real humans, do their work better.

We, the B2B folk, are interconnected. Our cosmos is how society works. All our organizations and networks are minicommunities in themselves. Sales and marketing must have absolute clarity about the role we play and the value we create in our neck of the woods.

Since we've clarified that we are talking about people and not concrete buildings, then we must think how our buyers think and go where our buyers go. Know that your buyers are not buying a product or service from you; they are buying a solution to a problem or a tool to achieve a goal. The better you are at clarifying the problem you solve—and exactly why your customers choose you—the sharper you can hone your marketing message to repeat those ideal engagements.

> Everyone is not your customer.
> —Seth Godin

The worst thing you can do is try to serve everyone. This never works. It only waters down your message and slows down your sales cycle. I don't care if your product can help everyone; your organization can't. You have a culture, an approach to customer service, efficiencies, and even flaws that will not be suited to an entire market. The Pareto principle, developed by economist Vilfredo Pareto, asserts that 80 percent of our outputs (or consequences) come from 20 percent of the inputs (or causes). This 80/20 rule suggests an unequal relationship between inputs and outputs. Only certain inputs—the vital few—will create maximum results. I have found that this principle frequently applies to the levels of business development. If you check your own numbers, you might find that

- 80 percent of your sales will come from 20 percent of your customers,

- 80 percent of your sales will come from 20 percent of your sales team, or
- 80 percent of your profits will come from 20 percent of your contracts.

This is key to prioritizing the right things. When looking at your market, focus on who the 20 percent are, specialize in them, and serve them to a masterful level. This is how you build scalable, repeatable, and predictable success and growth. It does not take all the buyers to be successful. It takes the right ones. Often, what you actually need in order to hit your growth goals is much smaller than what you'd think. If I'm hungry, I'd rather fish in a barrel than fish in the open sea any day. This is the key to continually finding ways to cut waste from your marketing spend and your sales process.

> If you aim at nothing, you'll hit it every time.
> .—Zig Ziglar

Messaging on a Personal Level

The average B2B sale has eight decision makers or influencers. Executives today are more likely to desire consensus over unilateral decision-making. Despite the fact that these decision makers work for the same company and are reviewing the same purchase, their personal agendas can be wildly different. For example, let's imagine that a division manager, a purchasing agent, and a CEO are the key decision makers.

The division manager cares about the service level of the selling company, the overall impact on his team's work, and how hard the transition will be once the new solution is put in place. He probably worries about how this will affect his reputation and maybe even his job security.

The purchasing agent is incentivized and accountable for monitoring margins and keeping costs low.

The CEO knows about the acquisition strategy that hasn't yet begun and is secretly evaluating whether the solution will be scalable and appropriate for the acquired companies in the future.

Additionally, these three individuals prefer very different types of information and styles of communication to help them make decisions. A cookie-cutter value proposition simply won't work for the division manager, purchasing agent, and CEO in this one sales opportunity, let alone on a broader scale.

As a marketing agency, we *never* skip the discussion about who the ideal buyers are. To create resonant messaging, to build a highly effective marketing plan, and to stand out in a sea of sameness, *we must place the humanity of our buyers at the center of our business-development approach.* Being good to others is the cornerstone—in marketing as in life. And if that's too fluffy for you, I'll give you another reason: you simply do not have the money, time, and attention to reach everyone.

So how do you clarify, find, and specialize in the right segments of your target market? You identify the personas of the people who make or break your success. You must know your audience to predict how they will respond to what you have to offer. In marketing jargon, this is called documenting your *buyer personas*. How can documenting your buyer personas help you?

- It dramatically increases leads by using insights that you know will trigger interest and action.
- It helps you find and retain more of the right type of customers.
- It guides you on how to speak your customers' language and encourage engagement.
- It leads your company to be more buyer driven, with messages, content, products, and services designed to serve your market.
- It helps you and your team make better budget-based decisions by creating decision-making criteria based on attracting your ideal customer.

> Your audience is one single reader. I have found that sometimes it helps to pick out one person—a real person you know, or an imagined person—and write to that one.
> —John Steinbeck

In order to understand buyer personas, let's first talk about what they are *not*. Often, when I ask people to describe their buyer personas, they'll name an industry, a vertical, a size of company, or any number of equally broad terms. They'll say, "We work with small and midsize businesses." Hmm … as of 2018, there were 30.2 million small businesses in the United States alone, with almost 59 million people employed by them.[20] Where would you even start? Very few companies have budgets large enough to be impactful with an audience this large.

Or I'll hear people say, "We work with original equipment manufacturers." This term is so broad you can't even quantify what it means. I know this personally because I work with a lot of original equipment manufacturers. Some of them manufacture aircraft landing gear while others manufacture lawn chair parts. I assure you that they care about very different things.

If this is how you view your market, you're not specializing, let alone humanizing those you serve. If you can't clearly communicate who you serve, you'll not only struggle to clarify your value proposition to prospects but also have a difficult time helping your employees understand your mission, what you stand for, and how to best serve your customers.

Buyer personas are typical snapshots of your ideal buyers. Most organizations have more than one ideal buyer persona. These profiles will help you identify how your ideal buyers weigh their options, what they worry about, and what their day-to-day lives look like, as well as their attitudes and preferences. From this information, you can develop plans to convincingly convey why they should choose you instead of your competitor or even instead of maintaining their status quo. Segmenting and clarifying your key customer types lets you enter your buyers' mindsets; you understand how they buy and gain insights on how to best appeal to their goals and motivations. Additionally, clarifying these personas will help you more effectively marshal your resources for maximum impact.

So if your goal is to sell more and dominate your market, knowing what types of people you are speaking to is critical. This helps you create agreement across leadership, marketing, and sales to develop targeted messages that sell and to match them to the right tactics.

If you google the definition of *buyer persona*, you'll find heavy hitters from all avenues of communication toting the importance and power of taking the time to know your audience.

It's the magic behind successful movies, brilliant speeches, great stand-up comedy, galvanizing politics, and other forms of communication. You have to know your audience in order to know and direct what type of reaction you want to get from them.

Buyer personas are the first piece of decision-making criteria in your marketing strategy. Anytime you are considering what to spend money, time, and attention on, you can use the insights you have about your ideal customers and ask yourself, "Does this help us help them?" This alone will help you separate the good marketing tactics from the ones that simply won't work for you.

Buyer personas simply make sense. They help you find your best customers—and vice versa. Your marketing strategy is more efficient, and you don't waste time chasing uninterested leads.

Because today's B2B buyers are savvier than ever, they are always looking to be educated and informed at each stage of their buying journey. Whoever crafts their messaging according to what buyers are researching and asking themselves ultimately wins the conversion game.

Going through the buyer-persona process is a powerful ingredient in your overall strategy.

Developing Your Buyer Personas

The average B2B company or division has three to four ideal-buyer personas.

So how do you develop personas that represent your best buyers? You can construct or document your buyer personas by tapping into the tribal knowledge of your client-facing employees and also through market research. Strong buyer-persona profiles are based on two data-gathering methods: (1) external intel and (2) internal intel.

External Intel: Ask your customers! Harvesting insights from your actual customer base gives you firsthand information about their personas, wants, needs, and intentions—things you want the right answers to. Surveys and interviews (e.g., "voice of the customer" insights) are two common tools for this type of research, which marketers agree are highly effective in encouraging buyers to tell their stories.

Studies show that companies who have moved toward buyer centricity consistently outperform their competitors:

- Companies who exceed lead and revenue goals are more than twice as likely to create personas than companies who miss these goals.[21]
- Seventy-one percent of companies who exceed revenue and lead goals have documented personas.[22]
- Using marketing personas made websites two to five times more effective and easier for targeted users to navigate.[23]
- Buyers are 48 percent more likely to consider solution providers that personalize their marketing to address their specific business issues.[24]
- Ninety-three percent of companies who exceed lead and revenue goals report segmenting their database with personas.[25]
- Fifty-six percent of companies have created higher-quality leads using personas.[26]
- Thirty-six percent of companies have created shorter sales cycles using personas.[27]

Some companies do face-to-face interviews, while others turn to inbound marketing to let prospects group themselves according to their personas. Have you ever come across an online form asking you, "How would you best describe yourself?" This is one reliable tactic to get persona data.

Internal Intel: Many B2B companies don't have the resources (or the appetite) to conduct comprehensive research, surveys, and interviews, so a good alternative is to gather data through the experience and knowledge of your top salespeople and client-facing employees. They are regularly in contact with your customers, so developing personas based on their qualitative assessments will greatly help you market your products and services accordingly. In order for you to get a 360-degree view, these discussions should include experts from sales, operations, customer service, and marketing. It's remarkable what happens when the insights from one division are uncovered and found to correlate with the insights from another. Clear, unique areas where you can bring additional value to your buyers begin to show themselves. Unless you maintain an up-to-date record of buyer personas, the market knowledge your team has is not available on an organizational level. Harvesting your best people's insights and experience into your marketing strategy via buyer personas gives you the intel on what you should be communicating across your entire organization. Just remember that you must intentionally distribute this information across all levels of your organization to develop a customer-centric organization.

Because buyer personas are the types of buyers you want to work with, you must be sure to complete both demographic and psychographic insights. Demographics tell you who your buyers are while psychographic information tells you why and how they buy. The latter can include buying habits, likes and dislikes, and values. Both data sets give you a clear picture of your buyer personas, making them more relatable to the people on your team.

I recommend that your buyer-persona profiles include details on who the individuals of the identified group really are, their work identity, their agenda, and why they'll love you.

Who They Are

- demographics: age, gender, income level, where they live (urban, suburban, rural)
- day-to-day lifestyle: married, kids, typical work hours, personal responsibilities, favorite hobbies or escapes

- what situations make them nervous and what personal fears keep them up at night
- personality and communication style

Their Work Identity

- job details: position, role, responsibilities
- background: education, typical career path
- pain points: business issues, risks, or concerns
- goals: what they want to achieve, experience, etc.
- attitudes: buying preferences, motivations
- main sources of information: where they do most of their research and reading
- what makes them nervous and what keeps them up at night
- how they like to receive information (data, stories, videos, graphics, etc.)

Their Agenda

- their level of security in their role, what they are accountable for, the metrics they use
- where are they in their career journey, what they may be protecting
- what could get them fired
- who has ability to say yes, who their trusted advisers are
- their biggest fear or frustration at work

Why They'll Love You

- how you can help them get what they want
- how your company and offering uniquely align with what they care about
- the business problem you can solve for them
- what they are unable to achieve because of this problem
- the wider impact of this problem on their team or organization
- the emotional problem you can solve
- what are you competing with, besides your direct competitors (inertia, fear of change, other business options, etc.)

Sample Documented Buyer Persona

> **Demographic Information**
> -executive vice president
> -male
> -late forties or early fifties
> -charismatic, likable
> -incredibly busy, work-life balance may be a problem
> -travels a lot
>
> **Psychographic Information**
> -needs to hit aggressive goals
> -must influence CEO to get support on initiatives
> -wants success at work but also a healthy lifestyle
> -tends to read or research a lot before buying a product
> -has tendency to pay more money for quality

Using Buyer Personas

As I mentioned before, your buyer personas are decision-making criteria, not a fluffy feel-good exercise. Your buyer-persona documentation should help you decide what to say, how to say it, and where to distribute that message. In short, *it should help you go where your buyers go*—physically, mentally, and emotionally.

What does this mean—to go where your buyers go? It means you must think like them as human beings and show up in the places where they live, work, and think. For example, lifestyles matter, because if one of your key decision makers is a working mom, you don't invite her to an evening cocktail event; she won't be able to make it, because she'll likely be picking up her kids from their caregiver. Many busy executives often spend a few hours working early on Saturday mornings. If your decision makers do this, then publishing or emailing content late on Friday or early on Saturday might be ideal because they're in work mode but conducting business at a more leisurely pace.

Consider, too, where your people get their advice when they are struggling with a decision. Do they use Google, go to their trade association, ask peers, pull up YouTube, listen to a podcast, or consult their

CPAs? You can develop amazingly creative and enjoyable campaigns if you know where to focus your attention.

A consultant who I worked with realized that his buyer personas sought insight from church friends and their CPAs, so he developed a Christian business program for churches to host, and he focuses on how he can help CPAs to be successful. Because these people know him, trust him, and actively seek out his counsel, they know they can refer him in integrity.

When I say, "Go where your buyers go," I'm referring to walking in their shoes. You must learn to think and feel what they think and feel.

As you begin to cobble together the right tactics and form them into a cohesive marketing plan, you can rely on your buyer insights to dictate even the granular details. This requires hitting the Pause button on your goals and your needs to dive into theirs. Your buyers don't care about your revenue growth, sales goals, or visibility. They care about doing their jobs, staying employed, achieving their goals, and trying to live lives that are more joyful than chaotic.

Answer the Ws through *your buyers'* eyes.
- Who do they listen to, care about, and trust?
- What do they want? What questions do they need answered?
- Where do they go for information?
- When do they need different types of information?
- Why do they (i.e., what triggers them to) take action?
- What is their problem preventing them from doing?

This last question comes from some of the best sales trainers on the planet, and it's equally important to your marketing. Usually, people know they want to solve their problem, but they need something important enough to convince them to make a change and take action. For instance, if you sell something that helps leaders optimize their teams, the cost of inaction might be that they can't take the vacations they want to, or because of all the people problems, they can't find the spaces in their calendars to launch new offerings. If you sell something that reduces risk, you might be helping them to stop procrastinating on key decisions. If you sell something that helps people to be more successful, then you might actually be helping them to get more speaking events, travel more, save for vacation homes, sell their businesses, or buy red-bottomed shoes. What's the full story of the people you are trying to serve?

If you don't know where they are and what they value, you cannot bring them value. B2B buyers continue to desire more value and have higher expectations of sellers, and according to surveys, they are increasingly disappointed. Less than a quarter (23 percent) of buyers select vendor salespeople as a top 3 resource to solve business problems.

If you're ready to stop wondering whether your marketing will work or whether you're wasting money, documenting your buyer personas will answer those questions. Only go to the places, only spend on the tactics, and only talk about the topics that your buyers care about.

You can download a buyer-persona worksheet at DaciaCoffey.com I highly recommend you do this with a cross-divisional stakeholder team of three to ten people. This information should become decision-making criteria. Now let's begin putting this information to good use.

> **Negative Personas**
>
> For some organizations, it can also be helpful to document the one buyer persona that kills your profit and joy. If you have a type of buyer you keep attracting to your own detriment, you can employ these same insights to avoid these business leeches and focus on the buyers who propel your success, not derail it.

The Rearview Mirror

- Knowing your best buyers intimately is the single most important aspect of your marketing and growth strategy.
- Buyer-persona insights help you develop the right message and choose the right tactics, which will accelerate your results and maximize your resources.
- You can gather these insights through external or internal means.
- Your buyer-persona profiles should include both demographic and psychographic information.
- These documented insights should form the basis of your marketing decisions and business-development style.

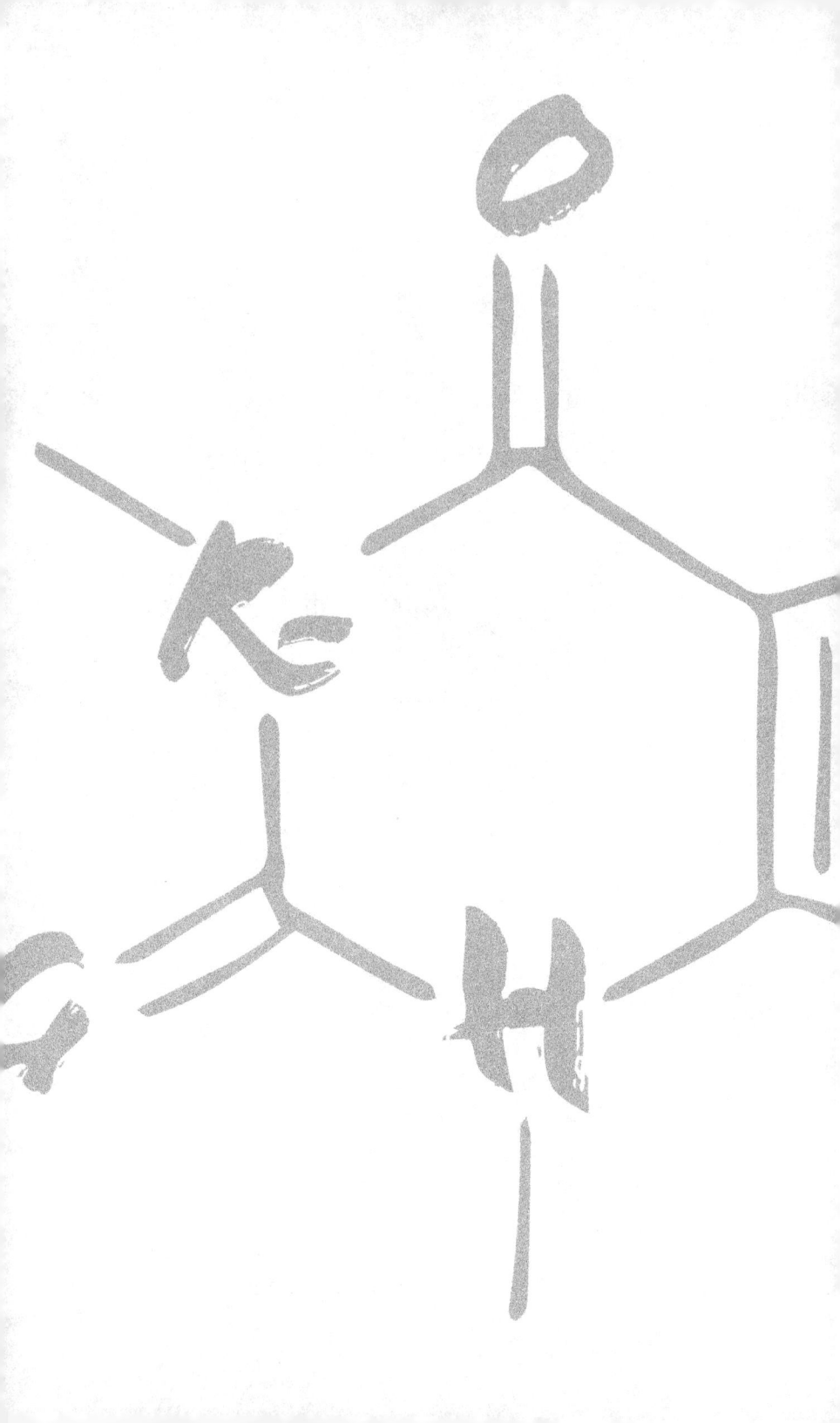

4

EFFECTIVE MARKETING PLANS MADE EASY

Marketing plans can be complicated and cumbersome to put together. After all, you're trying to align the prospect, the salesperson, and the marketer. However, there is a simple way to put the customer at the center and map the tactics that will help you create the success you are seeking.

Oftentimes, leaders and marketers alike get caught up in the tactics. Instead of their asking, "How do we leverage marketing to achieve our goals?" I hear questions like "Should we launch a new email newsletter?" and "Should we be on Instagram?" Or, worse, a leader will hear about something someone else is doing and bring this idea to the team to execute. This is the epitome of throwing something against the wall and hoping it will stick. Some of your initiatives will work, but without a structured approach to marketing decisions, you won't know why. This is further complicated by the fact that, every month, hundreds of new platforms, media outlets, influencers, technologies, and the like emerge to "help" you reach your target market. In 2011, there were 150 technologies available to sophisticate your marketing efforts. Today, there are more than 8,000 and growing. When you add the number of media outlets, events, digital platforms, and endless creative ways to distribute your brand name and message, the volume of options can feel less like a mountaintop from which to shout your name and more like a landslide that will suffocate you and your message.

This is where your marketing plan should assist you—except that, often, marketing plans aren't actually helpful. You'll find an endless variety of explanations through Google for what should be in a marketing plan and how it should be formatted. But you're not looking for a pretty document; you're looking for a plan that keeps everyone on track to make money. Instead of a massive report that reads more like a business description than a marketing plan, your marketing plan should simply state who will buy from you, why they'll buy from you, and how you'll get that message to them so that they do buy.

No more tomes collecting dust instead of dollars. Instead, I advocate for two documents that your marketing team should reference weekly, if not daily. You'll have a marketing-strategy document that includes your buyer personas, key messaging, and brand truth as your decision-making criteria (we'll cover messaging and branding in chapters 5 and 6). And you'll have an actionable document outlining your outreach as your tactical marketing plan. Your marketing strategy should encompass your decision-making criteria. Your tactical marketing plan should show how you will distribute your communication to your buyer personas.

So where do we begin? With buyer personas' preferences, of course. People love to buy but hate to be sold. This, in a nutshell, is why sales and marketing alignment is so critical. Because the only way to be aligned is to be absolutely focused on the customer. Marketing and selling must bring value to the buyer. It's a shift in thinking—a shift away from specializing in your product and toward specializing in your audience. As we discussed in the previous chapter, the real goal is to sell what your market is actually and already buying. Individuals are not buying products, services, features, or even benefits. They are buying a change that will make their lives easier, happier, or more profitable. They are buying forward progress. Period.

Sounds obvious, until you add the emotion behind revenue generation. Sales is the lifeblood of every company; if you can't close a deal, it doesn't matter how superior your mousetrap is. Sales is high stakes not only because most salespeople's potential income is based on how much they sell but because the stability and livelihood of everyone else at the company are also on the line. The sales life is one person going out there one day at a time, reaching out to one decision maker at a time, and closing one deal at a time—all while trying to hit an ever-increasing number. There is no finish line in sales *ever*.

Because of this, salespeople spend an inordinate amount of time thinking about how to be better than the competition, how to communicate value, and how to react to what a decision maker is saying, as well as focusing on doing anything it takes to move a prospect one step closer to a sale. Every conversation adds to their knowledge and arsenal of information to help them better advocate for their products, but it also makes salespeople insanely product focused. Salespeople champion "us," and this constant "why choose us" advocacy can make anyone myopic.

But when you embrace the idea that you are helping people to be more successful, you are forced to change how you approach business development. Sales and marketing alignment means embracing, throughout your entire organization, a servant-leadership mentality through which you teach your prospects how to make the best decision. Your legacy in turn will eventually be about the transformation you created for others. If you incorporate this endgame thinking into your day-to-day reality, it's not only the right thing to do for your market; it's the right thing to do to fulfill your potential and role in this world.

It is a relief for people, or buyers, to make a choice and move forward. They cross something off their lists and move out of indecision and into progress. And here's the rub: even though it's your product or service that creates the progress, it is your customer who gets and deserves the credit for it. As humans, we are the central characters of our own stories, so our business-development approach needs to reflect this truth. This is the hallmark of world-class business development.

In discussing his first principle in the book *Building a StoryBrand*, Donald Miller explains that "the customer is the hero of the story, not your brand. When we position our customer as the hero and ourselves as the guide, we will be recognized as a trusted resource to help them overcome their challenges."[28] Presentation and story expert Nancy Duarte teaches her clients to position themselves as Yoda and their clients as Luke Skywalker.[29] The best marketers and sellers in the world recognize that you don't do the work or achieve the results; you guide buyers to a new place where they win the day.

This approach is strategic, not tactical, in nature. It requires the creation of an orchestrated series of sales engagements that confirm the prospect's need for improvement and teaches the client how to make a great decision. In the book *Lean Selling*, Robert J. Pryor advocates for a selling approach that eliminates any activity from the selling process that, *from the customer's perspective*, does not add value. He challenges, "Why is it that we provide a service to Customers but not Buyers?"[30] He goes on to explain that buyers and sellers have common ground on which to collaborate and that it is possible for the seller to act like a coach to help the buyer make the best decision possible in the most efficient manner.

Maybe this sounds obvious to you, but ensuring this is a reality throughout your organization is not so easy. Simply communicating these nice sentiments doesn't change sales behavior, and it doesn't improve marketing execution to better support sales. Why is alignment across sales and marketing and across the chasm from buyer to seller so difficult to achieve? Well, simply put, our natural inclination as humans to focus on our own needs and desires puts us at cross-purposes when we communicate.

Let's explore what this looks like, based on what I've heard from different people in the buying-selling dance. When making a purchase, buyers progress through stages that we might characterize as follows:

- **Awareness:** "I have a problem, and I'm frustrated, and it's affecting my ability to do my work without hassle. What can I do, and how am I going to find the time to figure this out?"
- **Consideration:** "I need options and am figuring out on my own which ones might work for me. I don't want a salesperson wasting my time."
- **Decision:** "I see the light and have a pretty good idea of what I want and how it will make us more efficient and give us a

competitive advantage. Now I just have to pick the right provider, build consensus, and not get screwed."

To buyers, they are in control during the awareness stage because they are simply researching their problem. They are curious and maybe even excited that they are going to solve a problem once and for all. But as they progress through the process, or move toward a final decision, they come closer to parting with their money—and closer to potentially making the wrong choice. As their journey progresses, they move from excitement to fear.

Salespeople, on the other hand, when trying to engage a buyer, enter the buying process more on the side of fear or discomfort. After all, cold-calling can feel like nagging and interrupting. They can feel like they're a nuisance because the buyers don't yet prioritize their problem over other projects. But as the sales cycle progresses, the process gets more exciting and fun. This is what I hear salespeople say:

- **Awareness:** "I hate prospecting and don't have time for this. I feel like my outreach just falls on deaf ears and only prevents me from working deals that are already alive. I know I need to keep the pipeline full, but I need to focus on my other opportunities."
- **Consideration:** "I'm so excited to be speaking with the buyer because I know that our offering is better than other options."
- **Decision:** "I need to hit my number, and this deal is mine to lose. I hope they close before month's end."

The increase in anticipation is at odds with how the buyer is likely feeling. As the sales rep gets more excited, the buyer is getting more nervous.

For marketers, building awareness campaigns can be fun, but trying to make the sales team happy can feel like grasping at straws in the dark. The work doesn't always feel fulfilling or effective. Worse, the organization is rarely able to correlate the direct impact of the marketer's work on the business, leaving them feeling undervalued. From marketers, I hear statements like these:

- **Awareness:** "We have to get our name out there and build brand awareness. We have lead-generation campaigns, social media and ad campaigns, and trade shows. What more does everyone want?

Of course, I can't prove that a customer came from a social media post."
- **Consideration:** "We have email campaigns in place, but it doesn't seem like sales is working the leads we're sending them. We don't have enough followers or engagement on social media, and sales doesn't do anything to help share the content. But we do have traffic to our website. Oh brother, sales is asking for *more* case studies, but they haven't given us any success stories."
- **Decision:** "Please use the most up-to-date proposal template. They are breaking our brand guidelines."

	AWARENESS	CONSIDERATION	DECISION
SALES	FEAR	FUN	EXCITEMENT
BUYER	CURIOSITY	WORK	FEAR

But here's the key: what might look like a natural and unsolvable problem of human nature actually represents a huge opportunity to structure your business development in a way that aligns these points of view. More important, this alignment will be dramatically different from how your competition is selling.

Let's look more closely at these different points of view and how you can align the buyer's journey, the sales cycle, and your marketing plan. It's critically important for you to understand that your prospects and clients are building a singular relationship with your company, not one relationship with sales and another with marketing.

Your buyers' touch points, or brand experiences, will come from different sources, but they add up to a single story. For instance, they google their problem and read one of your articles. They attend a trade show and speak with one of your reps. They receive an email from your company and unsubscribe. When they are finally ready to interview providers, they ask peers and do more googling. When they speak to a new sales rep, they confess that they can't remember where or how they know your name. After they have an initial call, they hit your website and look through any follow-ups the sales rep sends. As they get closer to a decision, they will continue to bounce among information from your sales, your website, any collateral pieces that are applicable, customer service or inside sales, and all the other marketing nurture points.

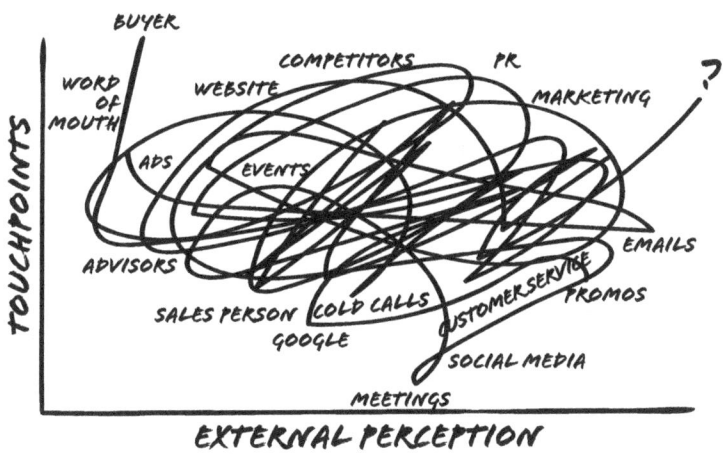

This culminates into one single judgment about whether your company is worthy of their business and loyalty. Ask yourself whether you feel confident that every touchpoint tells a consistent, helpful, and fascinating narrative orchestrated to help them make a great decision for their business. Or does it feel more like the chaos in the graphic? For most companies, each of these touchpoints is functionally separate. Inconsistency causes confusion (whether conscious or not), and it slows down decisions and waters down your ability to stand out from the competition. It's time to untangle the spaghetti. The buyer's journey centers around the question, How do I get from this frustrating place to a better future state? Buyers don't care—ever—about your product; they care only about *their lives* with it versus without it.

But what about a marketing cycle? We have a sales cycle and a buyer's journey. In theory, the marketing cycle is based on the buyer's journey, but not all consumer behavior, whether B2B or B2C, is linear. This is one of the challenges of marketing alignment, because without consistent words or even an openly acknowledged process you're driving forward, marketing can often feel like a never-ending experiment—one that permanently lacks any definitive set of insights.

As I mentioned in the introduction, my definition of *marketing* boils down to evoking desire in a specific audience, which leads to a sale. My next statement is likely to invite argument from my counterparts, and I say, "Bring it on!" because these discussions need to happen. So here goes. If we simplify how marketers evoke desire in a target audience, they basically have two tracks they must focus on: (1) the buyer's journey and (2) the comprehensive brand experience.

The buyer's journey is shown here in the traditional AIDA model: awareness, interest, desire, and action. While there are evolved versions of the model, the original suits our purposes for this discussion.

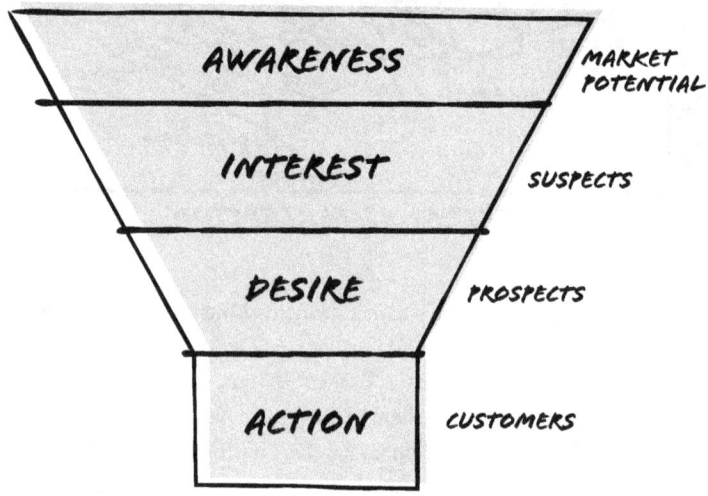

Marketers must develop messages and tactics to distribute to a wide audience of strangers to build awareness, or visibility, of their company and offering; generate interest in that offering; and evoke enough desire and trust that buyers take action and make a purchase. All of this work is *predictive*. Marketers study the market and buyers to make educated guesses about what will motivate people's buying decisions. *This is the logic side of the equation.*

Then marketers must manage the comprehensive brand experience. The brand strategy and customer experience really overlay AIDA and encompass the entire buying experience, from initial impression to customer delight and referral.

Marketers must translate buyer insight into messages (i.e., words, visuals, and experiences) that are distributed, or advertised, across multiple media both online and off-line; evolve to match the stage the buyers are in to nurture their interest; and then set up and track the data to test effectiveness—all typically without their ever being in front of a single prospect or customer. *This is the emotion side of the equation.*

Thus, marketers can get very focused on tactics, individual projects, and their individual metrics because there is a lot to juggle and just getting every piece out the door and working cohesively is a mammoth undertaking. So here, again, we see myopia because it's easier to get bogged down in the details than it is to return to looking at the system holistically to test for alignment with the buyer's emotions and the salesperson's actions. And when push comes to shove, marketers tend to align with buyers but miss the implications of the selling side. We see this in B2C commercials where the story line is touching or hilarious but the viewer later can't remember the actual brand behind the creativity. We also see this in B2B, where the calls to action are murky at best or missing completely. Thus, even if the buyer is curious, the lack of a clear next step fails to capitalize on the buyer's interest. The marketer forgets to guide the prospective buyer one more step toward the sale.

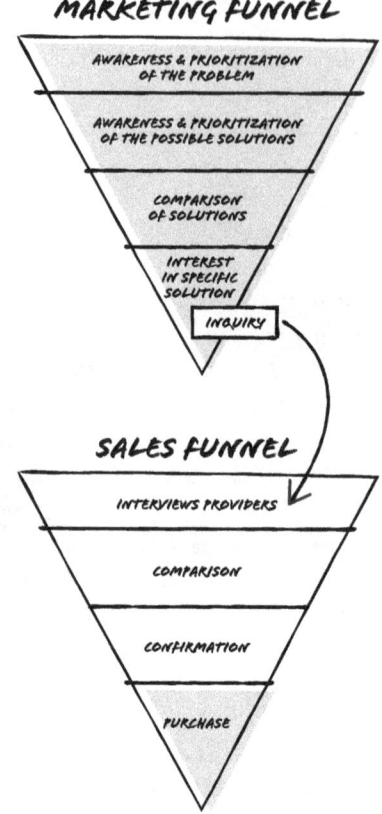

So let's look at how we, as guides, can map out a path for our customers while considering all three perspectives.

Using the Sales Cycle as a Map

While different sales training systems might use different semantics and a different number of phases, every sales cycle can be simplified into three phases. It's the salesperson's job to

1. generate interest,
2. build trust, and
3. close the deal.

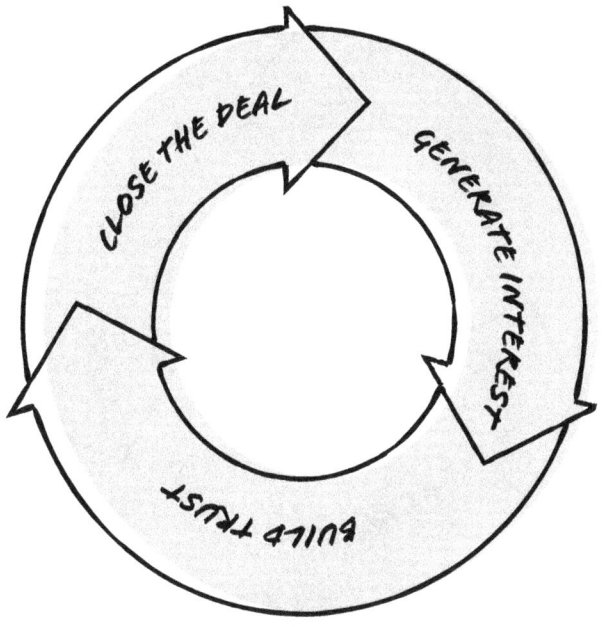

But the sales cycle has a sales point of view. In each phase, it instructs the action that the company or its representatives should take to bring in revenue. *Attract*, *build*, *close*—these are all words that prioritize the seller. This perspective is *not* customer centric.

What can get lost is the *real* thing a prospect is actually buying, such as peace of mind, lowered risk, time, competitive advantage, confidence, or money. There is always a time and a place to talk specifics and details, but you should never lose sight that your offering has to create a transformation from problem to solution for every single prospect.

The answer is to put the customer in the center of the sales cycle and map out what the salesperson needs to provide as they journey together toward a decision.

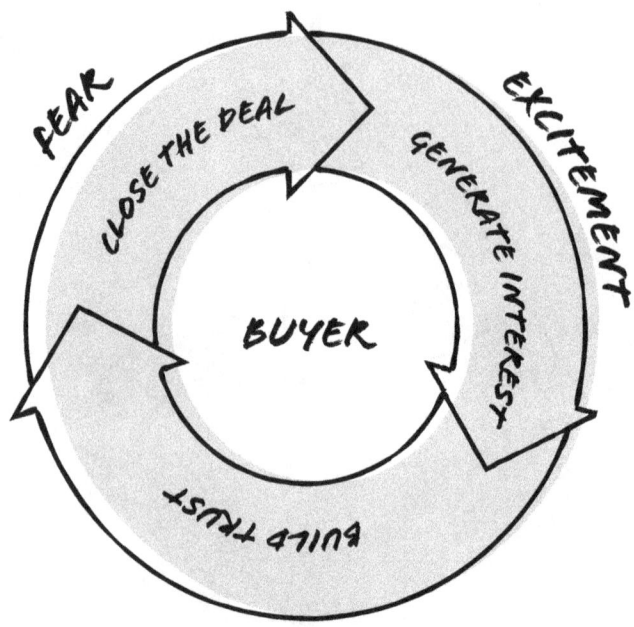

This means you create a map of tactics, processes, and tools for each of your buyer personas. Begin by choosing one of your buyer personas and drawing out the three stages of the sales cycle. The key is to look at what the prospect is doing, not what the salesperson is doing.

In the first phase, *generate interest*, you need to identify the channels through which your prospect may have heard about your company and what is happening in this person's world that made him or her curious about your offering. The prospect has become aware you exist, so what are you doing in your business-development activities to intentionally drive awareness? In sales language, you're generating interest; in your customers' language, they're becoming aware of their problem and possible solutions. Write down those tactics outside the *generate interest* portion of the graphic.

Here is a sample of tactics you might use to generate interest:

- advertising
- search engine marketing (e.g., Google Ads)
- search engine optimization
- cold-calling
- trade shows

- sponsorships
- referral programs
- direct mail
- signage and outdoor advertising
- radio
- TV
- social media
- public relations

Anything that puts your name in front of people who might buy from you to attract their interest belongs in this phase. For your planning, you will want to write down the tactics, tools, and actions for generating interest right on this section of the graphic. If you have ideas or plans for things you should implement, add them also.

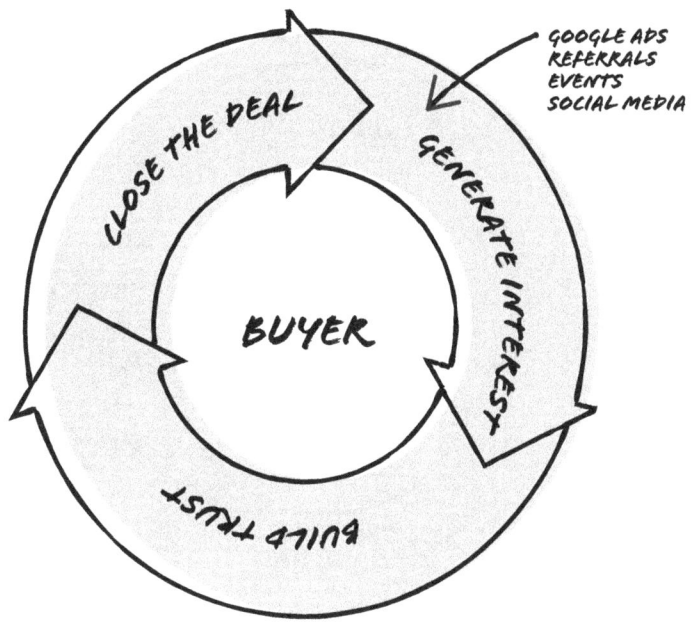

Next, we move on to *build trust*. This is where the prospects confirm in their own minds that you have a relevant solution they are interested in *and* that you are who you say you are. The buyers are now actively engaged in consideration of your product or service, and they want to make a good decision. They are asking themselves, "Are you who you say you are?" and looking for proof that you can be trusted. So if the sales language is to build trust, then the customer language is *consideration* of their options.

There are many tactics that serve to help you demonstrate worthiness and the options range based on your industry, but here are a few examples:

- website
- video
- demo
- sample
- testimonials
- case studies
- white papers
- research studies
- awards or recognition

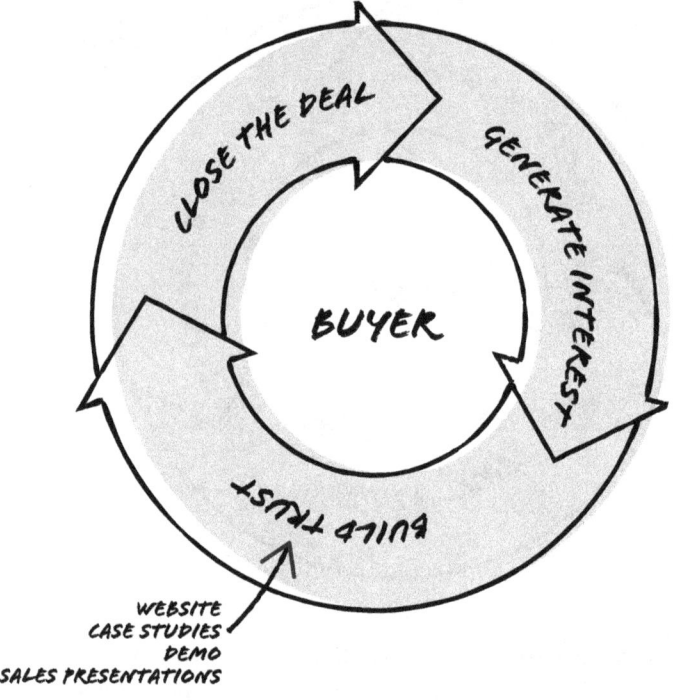

Close the deal is self-explanatory: your prospect chooses to do business with you. When executed well, this phase is a point of relief for both parties. The win for the salesperson is obvious. The buyers, on the other hand, are finally moving forward to solve a problem, but their journey is far from over. A new phase of their journey is just beginning, and it brings all types of new emotions and risks, like buyer's remorse, fear, change aversion, and change management, as well as finding time to implement the product or service, rolling it out to their team, gaining internal buy-in, and dealing with the actual implementation of your solution. Here, again, the sales language is *close the deal*, but the customer language is to make a *decision*.

This is most clearly the phase that the sales team owns; however, marketing can play a pivotal supporting role. So what tactics or tools are used in closing the deal?

- proposals
- live demos or free trials
- objection handling
- frequently asked questions
- technical review or audit
- requests-for-proposal responses
- diagnostic tools or assessments
- terms and conditions
- documented sales process
- pricing
- onboarding documents

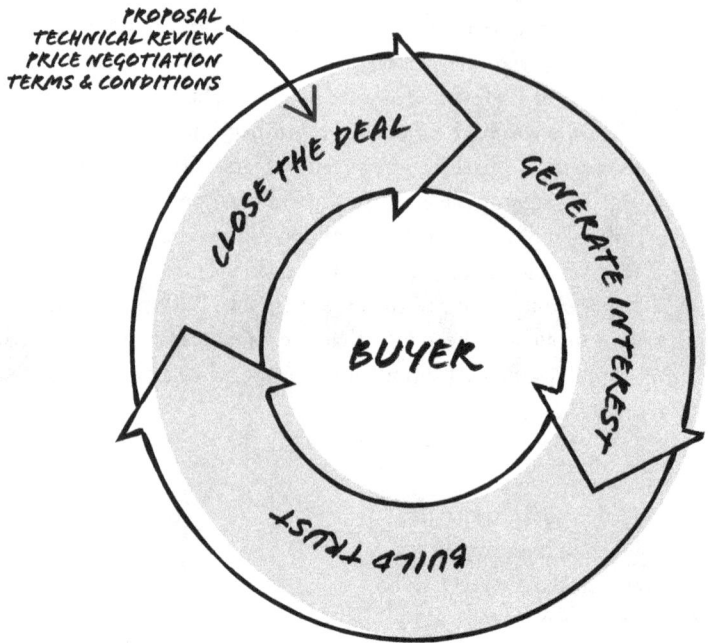

The reason we do this is so we can visualize the tactics matched to their roles in the buyer's journey. You can see where the bulk of your efforts are being applied and ask yourself whether your tactical decisions are appropriately aligned with the right challenges you face in reaching your market. Are your marketing and sales dollars solving the correct problem?

What you now have in front of you is your tactical marketing plan in a visual and useful format. But we're not done yet. We need to take a closer look at the execution of the tactics themselves and identify whether they are effective.

Exchanging More than Money

As you consider the buyer's experience of these tactics, it's critical to note that money you receive for your product or service is not the only transaction occurring. *Two additional exchanges happen in the sales cycle.* These exchanges push the buyer toward a decision and serve as the guiding criteria in the tactical execution.

Buyers are not idly sitting around waiting for something to catch their eye or spending hours reflecting on their need for your product. They are carrying on with their busy lives, buried in current projects, priorities, and personal agendas.

In all our business-development activities, we are actually asking our prospects to pull from one of their stores of limited resources: time, attention, and money. All three are either budgeted or squandered, and they add up to the quality of life a person leads. You are asking people to part with finite resources that they can never recoup, in order to prioritize your message and your company name above everything else on their plates at that moment in time. The exchange you're offering had better be good.

Let's take a look at each exchange. In the *generate interest* phase, you are asking a prospect to pay attention. You must create a message that is worth such a payment. I find that, generally, people pay attention to two things in marketing:

1. An empathetic experience. This is something that taps into their emotions and humanity and is a welcome break from their current activity because of the feelings you evoke. Think of humor, tearjerkers, curiosity, or intrigue (e.g., Bud Light commercials, movie trailers, celebrity sponsorships, etc.).
2. Validation. This happens when what you say confirms that the struggles they face, or their experiences, are not unique to them, and instead shows your prospects that they are not alone. Their challenge is not of their own shortcomings but a solvable external problem.

Both of these provide an emotional experience and align with either who they are (their identity) or what they believe (their point of view). *You are talking to them about them.* When attracting interest, you are asking for their conscious awareness and approval. This is the attention exchange. What are you offering that is so good they are willing to pay you from their bank of attention? This is the most difficult and expensive exchange, but without it, you cannot scale growth.

Dacia Coffey

The Exchange Is Attention ⇔ Emotion

If marketers are effective at achieving a great attention exchange, buyers will remember your name and what problem you solve, and they'll begin to associate their feelings with your brand. When you apply the tools, tactics, and processes in *generate interest*, the execution must be about the emotion of their situation. Once the attention exchange has occurred enough times and aligns (from a timing standpoint) with the buyer's needs or wants, the next phase begins: build trust.

In the sales-cycle language, the verb is active—to build, as if it's something one can do alone, but trust doesn't work like that. Maybe we use the word *build* because we'd like to think of trust as bricklaying, putting one credible act on another until a trust is built, but the reality is not like this. If you are building a wall with the proper tools and skill, the wall will eventually be erected. You simply lay one brick at a time. But if you're working to build trust, the other party can refuse your efforts. Imagine if you laid one brick at a time and someone stood right in front of you and removed the brick that you'd just laid. If the other person won't agree to leave the bricks in place, you might never build your wall. In short, trust requires collaboration. Both parties must build, placing trust in each other or extending trust to each other. Going back to our wall metaphor, you can extend the brick to the person before you, but it is he or she who must choose to lay it.

So when you are wanting to build trust with people, what are you asking of them? You're asking them to spend time in exchange for your expertise and guidance. The prospects in this phase acknowledge that they have a need or desire that you can fill, and as a provider, you are an expert on how to make the best decision to fulfill that need or desire. You have the ability to teach them how to be successful in this decision. (Spoiler alert: This is not selling. It's teaching—but more on that later.) You are asking them to spend time. Even our everyday words express the depletion of finite resources. You provide education and insight. They pay for it using their time to review your information.

The Exchange Is Time ⇔ Insight

When you apply the tools, tactics, and processes in *build trust*, the execution must be about delivering insight to help prospects make the best decision possible for their situation. Once the buyers have solidified their decision to make a purchase and you have proven your ability to solve their problem, we move into the *close the deal* phase. Again, you'll notice that the verb is a simple command: *close* the deal. Sounds as simple and straightforward as closing a door, but of course, this is not the case.

You're asking buyers to part with their money in exchange for your product or service. In making this ask, the salesperson must provide encouragement and reassurance. This is the place for not fear but total confidence. Addressing concerns and final questions calmly and clearly, reassuring the buyers of their good decision-making, and focusing on the rosy future of success will help to remove fear. These are the tools you bring to the table in this exchange. The buyer should feel confident that moving forward is better than inaction and that you are capable of orchestrating this change.

You are asking buyers to move from spending time to spending money. The buyers have a sunk cost in the time they have already committed to you to make this decision, so you could look at the close as two exchanges:

1. questions ⇔ confidence
2. money ⇔ product

When you apply the tools, tactics, and processes in *close the deal*, the execution must focus on removing buyers' fear, preventing buyers' remorse, and setting buyers up for success after they sign the contract.

At each stage of this unified approach, the buyers are central. Who are they, what are they experiencing right now, and what do they need to make progress? The salesperson reaches out to act as the liaison throughout the process, and marketing anticipates, develops, and distributes messages and tools to support this collaborative decision-making process.

If you look at the graphic, you'll see that on the outside are two phrases to remind us of the buyer's emotion. On the right side of the cycle is *create excitement*. The buyer feels relief, and possibly excitement, at finally solving a cumbersome problem. In these early stages, there is little risk, so it's comfortable for the buyer. However, as you progress and near *close the deal*, you read *remove fear*. This is because the investment is increasing and more doubts and concerns are creeping into the decision-making process. It is the seller's responsibility to help the buyer clearly identify the sources of concern and fear and honestly address them, collaborating on the solution. The best doesn't always win, but the best at removing fear does.

When you use your sales cycle to map how you guide a prospect to a decision, marketing and sales are not only on the same page but walking the walk of servant leadership before the sale has even been made, setting the stage for an amazing customer experience and even customer loyalty. Additionally, because your entire system is focused on providing prospects with what they need, when they need it, you make the sales process more efficient and often can speed up the time to close because you're not cluttering the process with unnecessary meetings, presentations, or information.

> It's worth noting that the salesperson's emotion is in direct contradiction to that of the buyer. Most salespeople feel fearful and uncomfortable trying to generate interest, but they increasingly become excited and confident when they prepare to close the deal, which might actually increase the buyer's fear!

Finally, if you have a vision or mission statement that extends beyond your corporate goals, this approach becomes missional because you can create impact and influence far beyond your customer base. In this approach, outstanding customer service begins *before* an invoice is issued.

We just talked about using your sales cycle as a map, so now let's talk about how to make sure you've identified the right tactics and explore some things you may not have thought of. It's time to put your marketing plan together.

Remember—your buyer personas form the foundation of your decision-making criteria. Your tactical marketing plan is your way to analyze options, prioritize the tactics that are right for you, and set your plan in an organized format to work from. After years of writing marketing plans, I've moved to a spreadsheet format for the tactics because it's actionable. You can download the template at DaciaCoffey.com.

SALES CYCLE	TACTICS	PRIORITY	BUYER PERSONA 1	BUYER PERSONA 2	BUYER PERSONA 3	NOTES
GENERATE INTEREST						
BUILD TRUST						
CLOSE THE DEAL						

Looking at the far-left column, you'll see that the marketing plan organizes the rows into the same phases we outlined in the sales mapping. Then, looking to the right, you'll see the second column has space to enter the tactics themselves, along with a column for prioritization and columns where you can enter the buyer personas. Recall your top buyer personas, and record one as the title for each of these columns.

Place the tactics, tools, and processes you identified in the sales-mapping activity in column 2 with the appropriate phase. Once you've entered all the tools and tactics, put an *X* under the buyer persona that this tactic is designated for. Several of your tactics will be appropriate for multiple buyer personas, while others will be right for only one. This helps you think through the execution of these tactics and, to some degree, your prioritization. When a tactic aligns with multiple buyer personas, recognize that this means you may need multiple campaigns in order to align the right messaging to each persona.

Once this is done, use an ABC rating system in column 3 to review each tactic and consider which once must be done first and is most critical in the short term. If a tactic aligns with multiple buyer personas, this might indicate that it's more important or effective than others, but that's not always the case. You can decide whether it will have a great impact on your goals; this format simply helps you to think critically in your decision-making.

Dacia Coffey

How Do I Know If We Missed Something?

The worry that there may be a breakthrough idea that your team didn't identify can feel stressful. How do you know that you got the plan right? Well, first recognize that your focus on buyer personas and your consistency will lead to results and improvements; it's never one particular idea that will make or break you. However, we do want to avoid business-as-usual thinking when putting these plans together. Usually, during the sales mapping, the new way to look at the progression through the sales cycle brings up new ideas and areas of inefficiency. But now it's time to step back and review the plan you've outlined to think creatively and critically about where the current hurdles are in your business development.

In *generate interest*, do you have enough visibility in your market? What is your competitive landscape? When you review the tactics, does your plan adequately address your need? If you already have significant name recognition, are you leveraging this, and where are the real bottlenecks? Where or why are you losing prospects?

In *build trust*, do you have good traffic to your site but no conversion? Are you able to get initial meetings with prospects but they stop responding to follow-ups and never move forward? Are your opportunities progressing through the pipeline in a predictable and efficient fashion, or do your sales projections constantly push to future dates? Do you have issues with not getting buy-in at the top?

During the *close the deal* phase, why are you losing deals? Where do you see frustration, friction, or delay from prospective customers? Are you losing work to unworthy competitors, or are you losing it because of indecision?

You'll want to think through the problems that are holding you back right now so you're clear on where to focus your time, attention, and money. When you narrow down the problems, you can hold additional brainstorming sessions or call on experts to reimagine how you approach these challenges. When you're building your tactical marketing plan, you must balance both long-term and short-term goals. Often, rapid results come not from the launch of a new idea but from optimizations of current efforts, such as improving targeting or conversion techniques, implementing sales training, catering messaging to specific buyer personas, and the like.

Review your plan and consider whether the tactics you've identified address the issues harming your progress, in addition to achieving the goals you've set. You will likely find a few places where you need to incorporate additional tactics or new ways to improve your overall business-development effectiveness.

Leaving No Stone Left Unturned

I look to two simple frameworks to help you ensure no stone is left unturned: (1) the seven fundamentals of a healthy marketing mix and (2) earned, owned, and paid media channels. A final assessment of your plan can include reviewing the fundamentals of a healthy marketing mix and asking yourself whether you've missed anything in each of these areas. At the end of the day, every single one of your options will still fall within one of the seven different categories. You can look at these elements and determine which areas you are strong or weak in to further validate the plan you are building:

1. Strategy
2. Brand
3. Website
4. Advertising
5. Digital marketing
6. Events
7. Sales and marketing alignment

The first three fundamentals make up your total strategic platform. The other four fundamentals are about distributing your message to turn strangers into prospects and prospects into clients. Can you see areas in which you need to be stronger, and have those been addressed in your plan? The Marketing Blender has built an assessment that you can take to help you identify where you stand today. You can find it at themarketingblender.com/assessment.

The second framework is related to your media mix and is common language to many marketers. This framework allows you to review the tactics in your *generate interest* phase, which is critical, as this is the most expensive aspect of your business development—and where a lot of waste and lost ROI can occur. You want to look at the balance in your tactics across earned, owned, and paid media channels.

What are these? Earned media is publicity or exposure that you didn't pay for. This includes nonpaid endorsements by influencers; shares and engagement on social media or forums; and mentions or appearances in magazines, on TV, or on blogs. Owned media is anything you have direct control over: your website and the content you create (e.g., blogs, videos, webinars, podcasts, case studies, assessments, emails, search engine optimization, etc.). Paid media is, of course, advertising you pay for, and it includes paid search advertising, ads on social media, print ads, commercials, sponsored content, sponsorships, and paid endorsements. By considering the blend of earned, owned, and paid media, you can oftentimes think creatively about avenues that you may not have considered in each of these categories.

Once you have reviewed and identified additional ideas, add them to the appropriate phase in the spreadsheet and prioritize your tactics. Remember that every one of your marketing tactics exists to increase your current and future sales opportunities by impacting buyers during the different phases of their decision-making process. Your goal is to design a robust ecosystem through which your prospects can engage with you—and find tremendous value during each engagement. It takes time and focus to create this ecosystem, and you must have room for evolution and improvement.

I want to add one reminder. No matter how diligent you are in this ideation, you may not think of everything, and you won't be aware of every possible option. That's OK. But when you put your plans in the framework I've outlined in this book, your results will improve. The key is to be clear on what problems you are solving in your business-development approach and to be intentional about going after them, instead of just chasing random tactics.

Now that your plan is in place, it's time to execute it, and the remainder of the book will focus on how to be irresistible and incomparable in your market.

The Rearview Mirror

- Putting the customer at the center of the sales cycle is critical.
- You can use your sales cycle to visualize or map what tactics you have in place and what they should be accomplishing while

you maintain alignment of the buyer, the salesperson, and the marketer.
- Each phase of the sales cycle—generate interest, build trust, close the deal—aligns with a specific exchange that should direct your execution of the tactics, processes, and tools.
- To build your marketing plan, you need to put your tactics from the sales-mapping exercise into a usable format. This is your tactical marketing plan.
- Match your buyer personas to your tactics and prioritize them based on your goals.
- To ensure you've considered the full range of your options, use the seven fundamentals and the earned, owned, and paid frameworks to brainstorm additional opportunities to improve your business development.
- Crafting your customer-centric approach before formal engagement can improve sales, set the stage for an outstanding customer experience, and increase your impact on the business world at large.

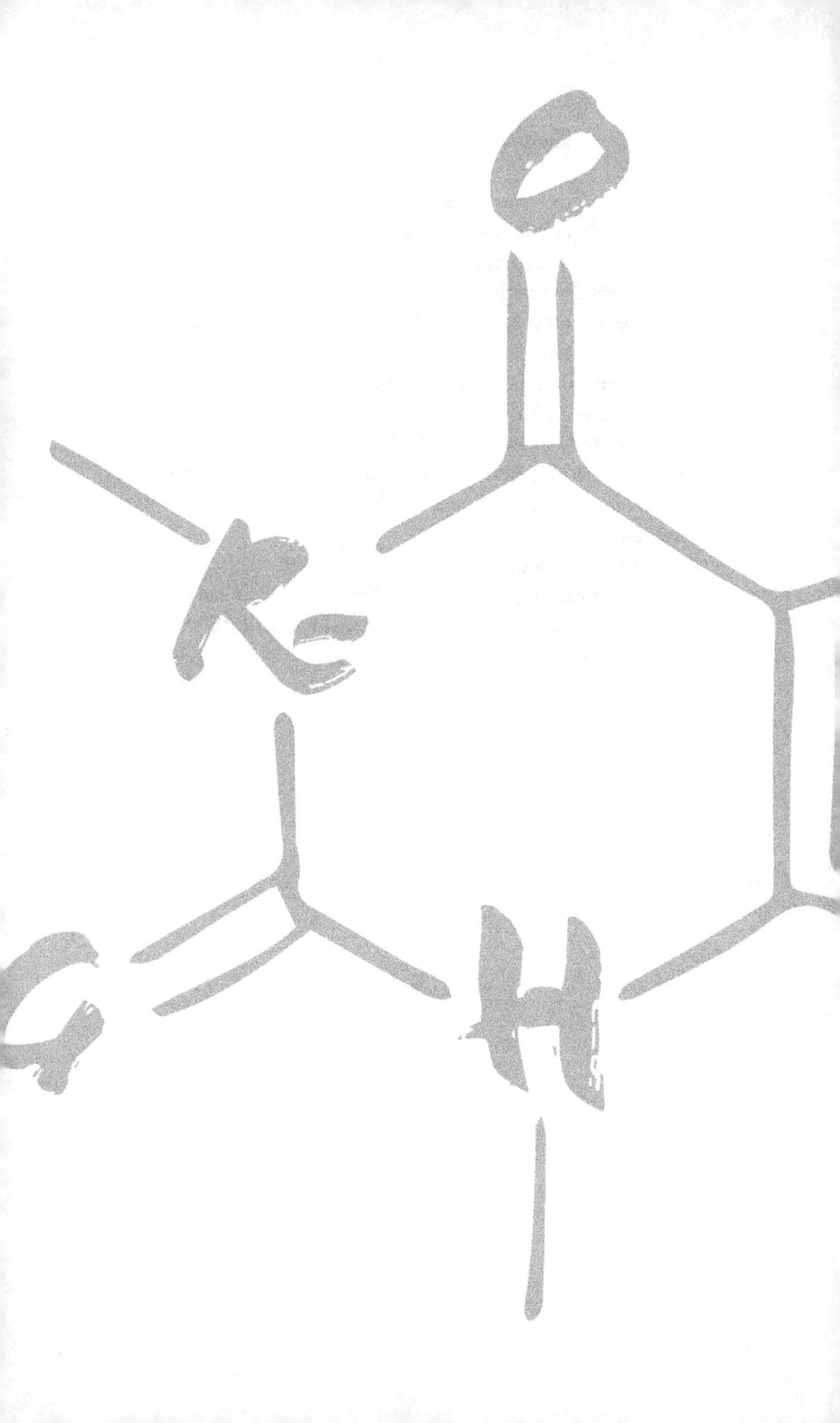

5
MESSAGING

Your business message should be a catalyst for action, not a handful of empty benefit statements. But messaging is not only about choosing the right words; it's also about organizing them in the same way that the brain processes information. You must say the right thing in the right order. The messaging-choreography framework can help you do just that and scale it across your entire organization.

Now that you've mapped your strategy and thought about how to prioritize and organize your execution, it's time to actually do it. Let's talk about how to choose the right words to convey and convince. Messaging is an art—one that is essential to your success.

The words you choose are critically important. They teach people to understand your truth and your value. They sell for you when you are not in the room. But more foundationally, your words bring things to life. Nothing can happen before you put an idea or a plan into words. Words are catalysts of action, seeds of inspiration, and conduits of understanding.

But all too often, words in business are just hot air. Because here's the truth we all know as listeners but don't accept as speakers: the fewer words you use, the better. This means that the words you choose had better be amazing, and they had better serve your listener and not just yourself.

This is why I've put the messaging chapter before branding. You must have clarity around what and why you are communicating. You need to have a plan to ensure that your words create the space for action instead of just expanding the buyer-seller void. In the busyness of business, I often see messaging turn into a last-minute afterthought, and then people are frustrated and surprised when their marketing tactics don't work.

Let's start with a simple rule of thumb: make sure your words serve instead of sell. Bland tactic-driven marketing doesn't work. If you want results, you have to take the time to know your audience, connect with them emotionally, and serve them well. What I see often is people's desire to chase a new tactic or add one more idea to the list, instead of going back and analyzing what is going right or wrong with their current efforts. We're so busy that we want to launch instead of plan—cross things off the list instead of building a successful framework. Working on foundational things, like messaging, doesn't always *feel* like progress. But we have many examples of how crucial it really is. A few years back, I worked with a financial-services company to build a better pitch deck for them because their prospects didn't see their value and weren't comprehending how the company was different. It took two months, and those in the company were frustrated. However, the first time they used the presentation, they landed the biggest client they'd had in their twenty years of business.

I've done quite a bit of work for companies in the infrastructure industry, especially around messaging, because it is a very tricky environment in which they must communicate to elected officials, consulting engineers, and contractors, all of whom have vastly different agendas. For example, when I worked with one tiny underperforming brand, we were able to go up against a Goliath and triple the brand's revenue in less than three years (without growing its sales team) by nailing its messaging.

Marketing is communication, plain and simple, but humans stink at this. Why? Because we all wear glasses colored by our perceptions, but not everyone's are rose colored. If you and I are having a conversation, what you say and what I hear are often very different things. There is the exact wording you use, the tone and cadence in which you deliver it, and the body language you employ, all of which is set in a specific time and space that give unstated context to the conversation. As your listener, I likely have preconceived opinions based on my experiences, which influence how I interpret your words. It's not hard to understand why I might derive a meaning very different from what you may have intended. The same thing happens in business communication. In marketing, you can promote your offering in the right place with the right amount of frequency and reach, and target the right audience, but if your message sucks, your results will suck too. The right message to the right audience wins every time.

Take the time to make your words count.

Without effective words, you can't do the following:

- delegate
- give feedback
- receive feedback
- set boundaries
- make plans
- collect insights
- get ideas
- share
- connect
- instruct
- lead
- influence
- ask
- learn
- contribute
- explain
- teach
- convince
- correct
- help
- sell

Your Messaging Choreography

People love to buy, but they hate to be sold. In *The New Solution Selling*, Keith M. Eades points out that making a purchase is a relief for buyers.[31] A purchase is progress toward a solution that helps them eliminate a problem or achieve a goal. Progress feels great, and it's critical for any great organization. Your product or service represents progress.

When you sell in technical or complicated environments, your role as marketer is especially important, as you must provide information that buyers need to know to make the best decision.

In B2B, we all sell to highly knowledgeable and often highly educated decision makers, but no matter how smart they are, you are the expert in your offering. Their businesses involve a huge range of expertise, and they simply don't have the time to specialize in your subject. If they did, they wouldn't need you. This gives you a unique opportunity to teach them how to make great decisions.

You see companies like theirs all the time. You see who is doing things well and who's not. You see how different customers are managing the trends and changes in the industry. You see who is winning. You may not realize it, but you actually own a mental map of your market—a big-picture overview of what it takes to thrive. If you can harness this tribal knowledge and shape it into a tool to serve your market, it can transform your positioning.

But here's the great thing: it can also transform your culture. When your messaging goes beyond the sale, you are arming every single person in your organization with the tools to positively impact your customers' lives and businesses. You are arming your people with the tools of increased meaning and increased influence in a very busy, dog-eat-dog world.

Serve; don't sell.

Every business ever created was built to serve. Even the most profit-minded businesses must help people get what they want or need. If you don't fill a need, you don't stay in business. We were all born to serve others—both as individuals and as organizations. Serve or die.

I employ an approach to messaging that can raise you above the fray not just because you'll be saying the right thing but because you'll be doing the right thing. In this messaging approach, you teach people how to make better decisions for their businesses, you find the point where you are incomparable, and you deliver this information in a way that truly resonates with people.

I call it *messaging choreography*. It draws from top-performing sales reps' insights and merges with behavioral-economics theory. In short, messaging choreography helps you organize your message in several ways:

- It helps you gain attention by aligning with what the brain decides is important.
- It provides context for comparison by reframing the decision through a bigger-picture lens.
- It leverages the power of story and data at the correct time in the decision-making process to position you as an expert and a trusted guide.
- It structures your message to embody your why in action by serving instead of selling.

The irony is that many salespeople employ the right information but often at the wrong time in the buyer's journey. Buyers simply will not retain or value information they receive at a time when it's not applicable.

So how does messaging choreography work?

1. We begin by mirroring the pains and desires of our audience to align with topics the brain has already deemed as important and is set to recognize.
2. Once we have established that our content is relevant specifically to the buyer's world, we teach the buyers that their struggles are not uncommon but in fact tied to larger trends beyond their control. I like to refer to this as *the big idea*. The big idea validates their situation and emotion but also reframes how they must view their decision. They are no long listening to a pitch from one vendor over another but benefiting from a guide who offers problem-solving options for dealing with a large and dangerous scenario.
3. We use stories and data to prove the truth of the scenario we have just shed light on.
4. Finally, we teach buyers what they need in order to overcome this challenge and how we are uniquely positioned to help them.

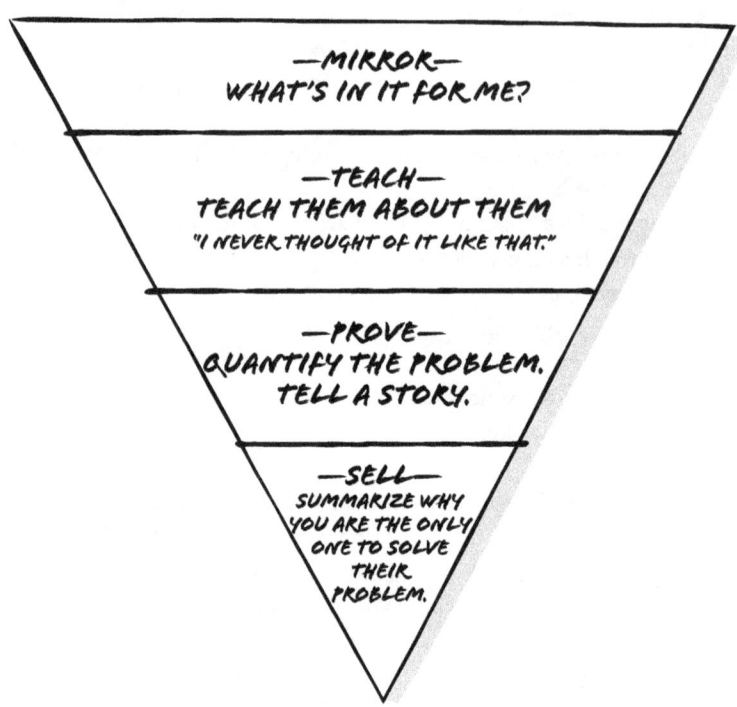

The wonderful thing about messaging choreography is that it holds your organization accountable for actually being a problem solver for your customers; you're not simply another vanilla provider trying to gain more market share. Messaging choreography requires empathy and an investment in time and attention to research the needs and pains of your market, build unique insights into how prospects can thrive, and communicate with vivid clarity and integrity when and how your company is the right choice.

Let's dive into each of the four aspects of messaging choreography: (1) mirror, (2) teach, (3) prove, and (4) sell.

Mirror: How to Get Attention

In such a busy world, people have the capacity to pay attention only to things related to their current lives and situations. Thus, the simplest approach to crafting relevant content is to talk about what people care about. Put another way, the number-one way to get people's attention is to talk to them about them. If your messaging can address what they care about, they'll automatically feel you understand them and can truly specialize in their specific problems and needs.

Begin your messaging by mirroring your prospect's state of mind. You want them to feel the emotional pain of their current situation when they engage with your marketing message. If there is no pain, there will be no change. A million things vie for decision makers' attention. Pain is what creates urgency and pushes them to prioritize one problem over another.

The pain of the status quo must be greater than the pain and cost of change. It's critical to remind prospects how difficult the status quo can be and what it's costing them. To do this, you must dive into your buyer-persona perspective. If you've done the work to understand their situation, your introduction will demonstrate that their problem is not singular but rather a solvable challenge that many share. You can even give examples from other clients.

Think of the flow of a great conversation you might have with a confidant or mentor. The conversation starts with your discussing the problem you have. Fruitful conversation follows when the listener responds first with "I know what you mean" and affirms he or she understands your point of view and your challenge. You're more likely to trust any insights or recommendations your confidant makes if you immediately feel that he or she is clear about your specific problem.

Most organizations skip this step completely in their marketing and sales approaches, which in turn puts the onus on buyers to find the company they believe best addresses their unique needs. Make it easy for them to put you on the short list of potential providers by helping them to quickly see that you specialize in them. Lead with empathy.

The biggest challenge here is to go beyond the shallow issues. In *The New Solution Selling*, Eades explains that pain flows through an organization.[32] Problems occurring in one area will impact people in other departments and teams, often resulting in a host of issues. The deeper the pain is felt, and openly acknowledged, the more the urgency prospects will have to buy. Decision-making occurs in the limbic system of the brain, which controls emotion. Truly powerful messaging leads with the language of decision-making—emotion—by uncovering the full extent of the problem and *how the problem feels*. If you want to stack the deck in your favor from the get-go, get to the heart of what they feel about their situation and what they fear when considering change.

Questions to Help You Mirror What Your Buyers Feel

- What do they really want?
- What is the theme of their job and their world?
- What are they really buying when they make decisions?
    - visibility
    - growth
    - productivity
    - ease of business / less hassle
    - more money
    - more sales
    - more influence
    - recognition and career building
    - support for their team
    - competitive advantage
    - fear removal
    - risk reduction
- Who else is impacted?
- What happens if they take no action?
- How much are these frustrations costing them?
- What does this problem prevent them from working on?

Teach: Communicate the Big Idea

Once you have built a connection through mirroring, your goal is to teach prospects something about their world that will help them. But let me be clear: you are *not* teaching them about your product or service. You are teaching them something new about their problem by connecting what they are experiencing to a larger problem in the industry or to trends exacerbating their problem. In essence, you are diagnosing the root of their problems.

This process of connecting the dots in a big-picture way not only provides a unique perspective on your prospect's problem but also validates their pain and frustration, as you're showing them that they are not alone in their struggles. You're saying, "This problem isn't completely your fault, and we've seen this enough to know that it's solvable." Whether they are time strapped, money strapped, or facing risk or uncertainty, you can provide additional information about what macrotrends are aggravating their personal situation. Chet Holmes, in his book, *The Ultimate Sales Machine*, refers to this teaching approach as "the science of setting the market's buying criteria."[33] As Holmes explains, "You will attract way more buyers if you are offering to teach them something than you will ever attract by simply trying to sell them your product or service."[34]

This is how you serve instead of sell. Validate buyers' experiences, show them why things are happening, and seek to teach them how to solve their problems. It takes discipline not to sell even one single advantage of your offering at this point, but remember that your job is to serve them in their buying process. Teach them how to make the best decision possible by giving them insight.

One point of caution: if you do this well, you are actually going to make your audience feel more discomfort. That's your job. If your buyer's problem is worth solving, you have to guide them past the busyness that can distract them from progress. No pain, no change—remember? You have to remind them of the pain they are in and then show them that it's not acceptable for them to remain in their current state. But building this teaching aspect is critical because its depth and effectiveness will determine whether you have a captivated audience or a captive audience (bored out of their minds).

Building the teaching aspect takes time and research and is a strategic initiative; this is not the type of thought and preparation you put off till the day before a big presentation. The marketing team—with proper customer insight from the sales team—should build this big idea and teach those in sales how to use it and apply it to their individual opportunities. It must align with the buyer's most frustrating or urgent challenges and teach them something new about why they struggle.

If teaching the big idea were distilled down into a headline or title, it might read like one of the following:

- The Five Ways Your Marketing Is Sabotaging Your Sales Growth
- The Hidden Costs Driving Up Your Operations and Administration
- The One Thing the Most Profitable Companies Know about Hiring Top Talent
- The Surprising and Common Distraction That's Killing Your Team's Productivity
- The Lurking Threat That's Already Stealing Your Customers
- The Early Warning Signs of an Impending Market Disruption
- The Three Insights That Can Double Your Profitability
- Five Ways to Cut Costs without Cutting People

When you can provide a new way to look at a current problem and put it in the context of a broader goal or struggle, you change the paradigm the buyer uses to make a final decision. It sets you apart and tees up your differentiation message. The buyer is no longer sitting through a sales pitch but engaging in strategic thinking and problem-solving.

Dacia Coffey

Prove: What to Say to Help Them Believe You

If you've done a good job teaching the big idea, you will have engaged your prospect's skeptical mind. This is excellent because it causes them to be curious or argumentative about your big-picture point of view, and when this happens, it means your prospects are paying close attention. Now you must back up your claims. You must share data and stories that demonstrate what you've taught them.

Many people in the B2B space are comfortable with proof and numbers, and many with analytical mindsets insist on quantifiable information. When you can support your insight with data, you will save people the time of having to research it on their own, and they will love you for it. If you've done the proper amount of thinking, you've likely pulled a number of reports, studies, or other sources to effectively communicate the big picture. Simply share the data points, your sources, and possibly even how your company came to realize this point of view.

But to truly hit a home run, remember that stories win the day. Our brains are wired to tell and understand stories. This is actually how memory works. Research suggests that facts are twenty times more likely to be remembered if they're part of a story and that people learn more effectively when listening to a well-constructed story. When you tell a story, you allow your audience to experience three different learning formats: (1) mental pictures, (2) your words and voice, and (3) emotional connections. Storytelling evokes empathy and takes the listener on a journey where pain and conflict are transformed into a desirable outcome.

By using quantifiable data, plus a key story (or two) that captures the emotion and reality of a situation, you build a messaging framework that is both believable and memorable. But let me remind you that the proof aspect supports your big idea; you have not yet earned the right to sell the advantages of your product or service. Stay in service to your audience. If you do, your audience will become curious about you on their own. Then and only then does your messaging become interesting to them. Your listener naturally begins to wonder why no one else has shed light on this subject in this way.

Sell: Communicating Your Incomparable Advantage

Now you have earned the right to sell. You've given your prospects value and progressed their understanding of their current situation. They are naturally going to want your expertise and will already suspect—correctly—that you know exactly how to solve the problem you just shed so much light on. So now it's time to outline what they need to solve the problem. I like the suggestion in Matthew Dixon and Brent Adamson's *The Challenger Sale*: create a list of what they need to solve or take advantage of the big idea. As the authors explain, "This is a point-by-point review of the specific capabilities they would need to ... make money, save money or mitigate the risk that you've just convinced them they're facing."[35]

After years of building these types of messaging scripts and training people how to use them, I find that this list acts as the perfect pause to keep you in an authentic servant-leadership posture. It also makes it easy for you to outline your differentiation message in a way that still maintains focus on your buyer's needs. This list becomes the distillation of your incomparable advantage. We'll go into how to clearly articulate and build your incomparable advantage in the next chapter, but the messaging choreography and big idea should dovetail right into the reasons why you are the only provider capable of handling the needs at hand and delivering real business impact.

Your incomparable advantage is not a better, faster, or cheaper value proposition but an explanation of your unique organizational characteristics, knowledge, and differentiators that culminate to clarify how you uniquely maximize value to your customers. Your incomparable advantage, as the name suggests, makes you distinct from others in your market, and your messaging choreography should help you navigate the conversation to a place *where there is no comparison*.

Having the discipline to save your value proposition until the end makes prospects more curious and attentive. Plus you can adapt their reactions and feedback to customize your message to their specific concerns. Curiosity will have led the audience to your differentiators.

As you consider your value proposition, it often helps to have tools to help you go deeper with regard to how your customers may perceive your incomparable advantage. An excellent resource for this is Bain & Company's forty elements of value that B2B offerings provide to customers, organized according to Maslow's hierarchy of needs.

If you truly want to be incomparable, you cannot stop at the words and phrases common to the business world today. *Efficiency, risk mitigation, cost savings, productivity,* and *customer-service excellence,* just to name a few, have become void of meaning because we all repeat the same words again and again. Take the time to identify the more meaningful, everyday impact of these value propositions.

While in theory your incomparable advantage may sound straightforward, I have found that clarifying your incomparable advantage can be incredibly difficult. So instead of diving deeper into explanation, let's take a look at how to work with your team to define this. Grab a whiteboard and your key team members, and do the following exercise.

Building Your Incomparable Advantage

List how you are better than every other vendor. Make a list of every single way you win for your customers.

After you list all your amazingness, go back to each item and ask yourself whether your competitors can say the same thing.

If the answer is no, put a star by the item and answer the following questions:

- What is the result of your competition not being able to do what you can do?
- How does the end user suffer without this feature or benefit?

If the answer is yes, then draw a line through it, because this indicates that the characteristic is table stakes—something you should be good at just to earn consideration. It's not a unique identifier, no matter how much pride you take it in.

If the answer is yes but you are truly better than your competition, then answer the following questions:

1. Specifically, what does the competition do compared to you? Where exactly are the differences in this common strength?
2. Do your prospects care about the preceding answers you listed? If not, answer why not. Either you will see missing areas where you can improve the big idea, or you will see that this benefit does not create value for your current market.

3. List three examples, details, or stories that demonstrate your superior delivery in this area.
4. How does this impact your customer's outcomes?

Review your list, and pull out the elements that your buyer persona would or should care about. These answers allow you to create two matching lists. The first is a list of the things your buyer persona should look for when choosing a provider. The second is that same list matched to the reasons you are the only one capable of providing this type of top-tier offering.

A Shortcut: Tell Transformation Stories

Recognizing that not every sales cycle includes a full presentation, I'd like to provide a shortcut on how to tell the full story in very short form. Remember you have to be aware of what your buyers are really buying. It's not your widget, your service, or even your expertise. They are buying a solution to a problem that is standing in the way of their potential. So the best way for you to communicate your trustworthiness is to tell a story about a transformation you played a part in. So what is a transformation story? It's a two-minute story about a customer who faced a problem similar to that of your prospect and what the outcome was after that customer worked with you. Stories serve instead of sell because they give listeners the freedom to place themselves in the narrative and to intuit what you do much faster than if they tried to understand everything only through product descriptions and value propositions. A great transformation story speaks to the heart of the purchasing decision. But it does not answer any questions about what you do or how you do it—it merely illustrates what transformation you created. Let's take a look at the elements of a transformation story.

1. Describe the person you helped. List the person's title and industry and any other characteristics that will help the listener understand your customer as a real person similar to him- or herself. This might include the number of size of the person's team; his or her experience, credentials, or personality; or even a tidbit about that person's work-life balance—anything that helps to set the stage for the intensity of frustration that client felt when you two first met. Here's what this might sound like:

To give you an idea of what we really do, let me tell you a quick story about one of our clients. A few years ago, I was introduced to a vice president of sales and marketing for a midsize manufacturer. He had built an impressive reputation in the industry and surprised everyone when he left the large company he worked for to join a company that was virtually unknown in the industry. It was his job to create a consistent business-development approach and message across the entire organization.

2. Describe the challenging situation the person faced that led him or her to you.

This company had no existing training, no consistent CRM usage, no website (no kidding!), and nearly zero name recognition despite forty years in business. They were invisible in the marketplace, the sales had plateaued in recent years, and several were now sliding backward.

3. Describe the transformation that occurred after you worked together.

Through our collaboration, our company helped them once again achieve double-digit growth year over year and have steadily built a market position based on authority and thought leadership. They are frequently featured in trade publications and have a strong and consistent market presence online and off-line, as well as the plan and technology to maintain this trajectory.

Your transformation story is an improvement on an elevator pitch. Everyone tries to get an elevator speech to be as short as possible—less time than you would ride in an elevator with someone, as the name suggests. But does this really serve the listener? Maybe giving yourself permission to speak for two minutes instead of only ten seconds could make all the difference.

Understand where your prospects are now and where they want to be, and then tell them a story that mirrors their desired goals. During sales mapping, we discussed the importance of keeping the customer at the center of your business-development approach. This is another example of remaining customer centric in action and not backsliding into your love of your own product and its advantages. By explaining the personal transformation of someone in a similar situation, transformation story once again answers the question, What's in it for me? Prospects can listen to your story and see their desired future state. I recommend capturing transformation stories in a short format, as shown in the chart that follows, and sharing them across your organization.

COMPANY & INDUSTRY	
TITLE OF DECISION MAKER	
SITUATION	
CRITICAL ISSUE	
REASONS	
DESIRED OUTCOMES	
WE PROVIDE	
RESULTS	

Your messaging is where your servant leadership takes life. The words you use either orient to a customer-centric approach or don't. When this happens, you open up a world of possibilities, innovations, and ideas for accelerating growth.

The Rearview Mirror

- Be intentional and proactive in building a messaging strategy.
- Using the messaging-choreography framework will help you to align with how the buyers receive information and will create consistency in the delivery of your message.
- Messaging choreography has four chronological aspects to help you gain attention: (1) mirror, (2) teach, (3) prove, and (4) sell.
- Mirror how your prospects feel about their current situation and problem.
- Teach them the big idea to help them better understand their problem.
- Prove the big idea with data and/or stories.
- To sell, match your incomparable advantage to the criteria your buyers need to solve their problem.
- Marketing should build the messaging choreography and assist in rolling it out to the organization.
- Transformation stories help to communicate your messaging choreography in a shorter format.

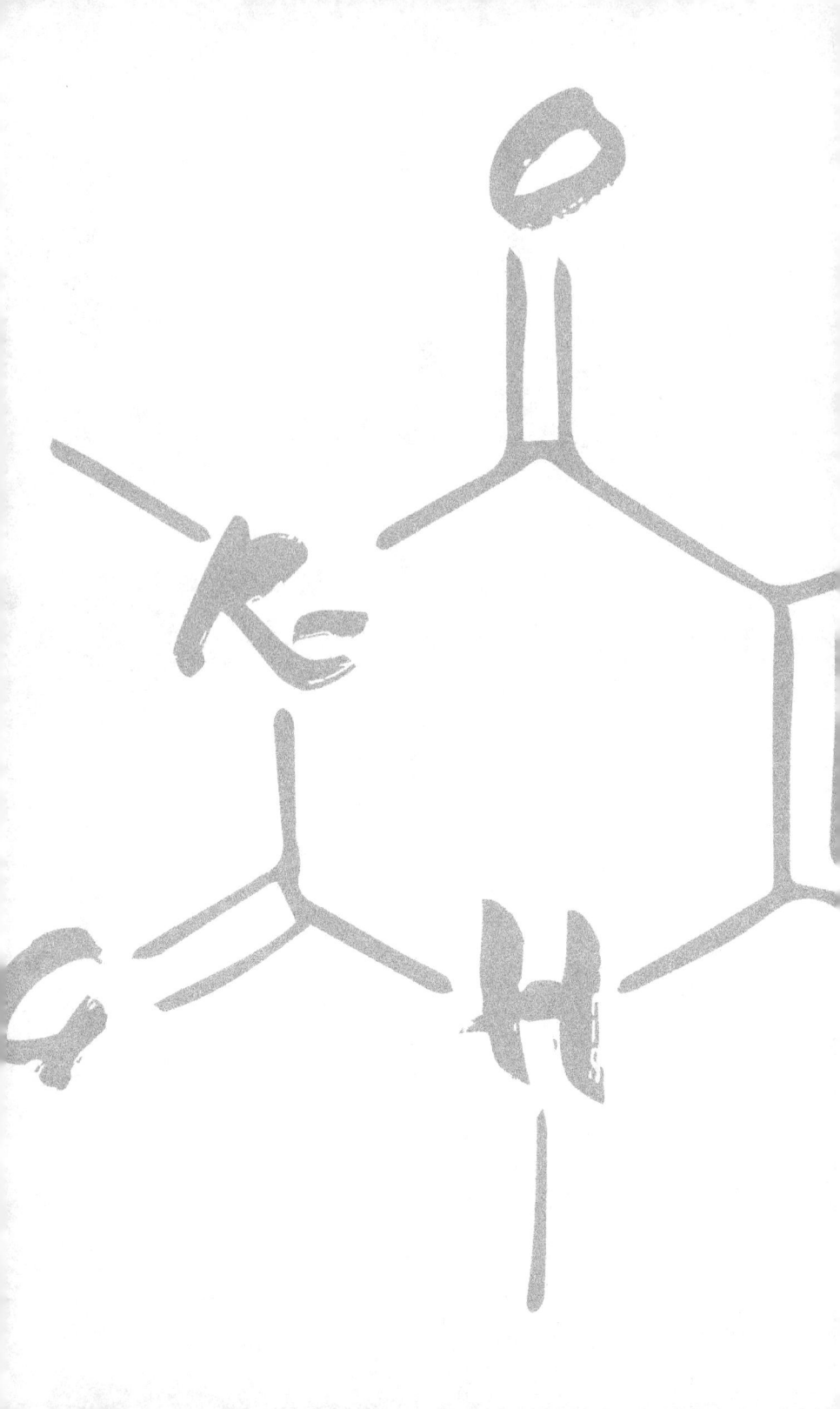

BUYING PSYCHOLOGY AND BRANDING

It would be impossible to build an effective business-development system without considering the psychology of buying and decision-making. The brain is complex, but understanding some fundamental principles can help create a more efficient buying-selling collaboration. Additionally, these insights, when merged with a few proven frameworks, can assist you in building a powerful brand that emanates the truth of your value, your culture, and your mission.

So we've talked about specializing in your audience and knowing the buyer personas that make or break your success. We've also visualized how marketing, sales, and the buying journey align. It's time to take these big-picture insights down to the one-to-one level, because the words and images you choose must lead *individuals* to decide to buy from you. Let's look at what's happening in an individual's brain during decision-making and how to apply the psychology of decision-making to help us better serve the prospective buyer. Get ready, because these insights are in direct contradiction to the way typical B2B marketing has been done in the past, but this approach is what will give your tactical execution real teeth.

We Are Not Logical

In 2002, Daniel Kahneman won the Noble Prize in economics for showing that humans don't make logical decisions, especially in the face of complex judgments. It was a shocking choice for the award, considering Kahneman is not an economist but a psychologist. Additionally, modern economic theory was primarily built on the assumption that humans are rational. As it turns out, we are not.

And this relates to the critical shift that must happen in B2B marketing. We cannot simply present complex information in a stack of logical bullet points and expect to win the day. Why? Because decision-making doesn't happen in the part of the brain that manages logic. It actually happens in the limbic brain, which is responsible for emotion. The *limbic system* is a collective term for brain structures that are involved in processing emotions, and it's responsible for all human behavior and decision-making and has no capacity for language. On top of that, this system processes information two hundred times faster than the cognitive brain! In other words, when we communicate merely the features, facts, and figures of a product, it doesn't catalyze action. This type of information only provides rationale for the decisions we have already made in the subconscious. Scientists have found that brain-damaged patients who have lost their capacity to feel emotion struggle to make even the most elementary decisions.

If you're like most of my clients, this just made you uncomfortable. Good. Do you want to know why your current marketing isn't working? Because you are not tapping into the most important tool in your marketing and in your humanity: your ability to create an emotional response in another person.

Let's think for a moment about what the brain is responsible for every day. The brain is responsible for keeping us alive; coordinating the body's systems; and translating impulses into movement, speech, thought, ideation, action, and emotions. It's responsible for subconscious processing, memory, learning, change, decision-making, and so much more.

Thus, a key function of the brain is to protect itself from overload and to pay attention to the right things, and it has a number of ways of doing this.

The brain is remarkable at preventing overload because it is a remarkable filter. Every second, we are bombarded by information. The human body sends eleven million bits of information per second to the brain for processing, and the conscious mind processes fifty bits of information per second. This filtering mechanism allows us to have a conversation in a crowded restaurant, drive a car, and pick up on peripheral danger signals. The brain is built to focus on the things of most importance and interest to us.

The key part of the brain that focuses attention is the reticular activating system (RAS). RAS is best known as a filter because it distinguishes between important information that requires attention and unimportant information that can be ignored. As Ruben Gonzalez explains in *The Courage to Succeed*, "Even though the cerebrum is the center of thought, it will not respond to a message unless the RAS allows it."[36] So what does the RAS let into the conscious mind? Ironically, only things that are already important. The RAS helps you decide what is important. For example, if you're considering buying a red Audi for the first time, all of a sudden, you will notice more red Audis than you ever knew existed. You will not notice black BMWs, yellow Volkswagens, or white Porsches. The RAS is also the part of the brain that recognizes your baby's cry or identifies danger. In short, the brain predecides what to pay attention to based on a combination of past experiences, life influences, desires, and one's current emotional state.

This insight puts a new twist on what you're actually competing against. Think about that for a moment: your message must contend for attention along with eleven million other bits of information per second. When you consider the three exchanges in the sales cycle, you are fighting for prioritization in your customer's mind. This means you're not just competing with your named customers. In the world of marketing and getting attention, you're literally competing with *everything* else your buyers see, think, and feel. You're competing with their spouses; their kids; the vacation planning to Disney World; the Bud Light they want after work; their email overload; and all the other wants, needs, problems, and interests they have.

And either your marketing message will trigger a predisposition for a buyer to pay attention to you, or it won't. Again, this is why it's so critical to know your buyer personas. If you don't know who they are inside their heads, you won't get in. This all happens in the subconscious and is related to getting people to know your name—that you even exist. This is what's happening in the attention exchange. Much of this book has been based on the critical truth that emotion drives decisions. Building your buyer personas will help you understand emotional buying motivations and how people's lives feel. Sales mapping helps you empathize with the emotion of the buyer's journey. Messaging choreography begins with emotion, validates, and gently leads them to a confident decision. Branding captures the emotion of your relationship to your customers. It is time for those in the B2B world to stop sabotaging their own efforts because they aren't comfortable with emotion.

The Brain Uses Shortcuts to Make Difficult Decisions

It's said that we make roughly ten thousand decisions per day, with 90 percent of our decisions made subconsciously. Complex tasks, such as learning, reasoning, and comprehending, which are conscious, call on a system of the brain known as *working memory*. Working memory assists us in executing tasks and controls our attention; it helps us hold on to information long enough for us to use it. But different tasks require different amounts of attention for successful completion, and working memory has limited capacity. This is referred to as *cognitive load*, and the working memory is extremely vulnerable to overload, as it can hold only around three or four bits of information at one time, and information in working memory lasts around ten seconds. In extremely complex situations, especially scenarios in which there is a lot of new information, our ability to learn and understand suffers. To protect itself from overload, the brain tries to reduce the effort associated with a task by using tried-and-true mental shortcuts called *heuristics*. Heuristics are simple and efficient rules that people use, whether intentionally or subconsciously, to facilitate their decision-making. However, they can lead to cognitive biases. By understanding common heuristics, you are better equipped to choose the right information to help decision makers during the buying journey.

Most decisions are influenced by the associations we've already made in the past and thus cue us to predispositions we aren't consciously aware of. Let's take a look at a few heuristics and how they align with the principles we've discussed thus far.

Repetition: Studies suggest that repetition can have a positive effect on someone's reception of, and agreement with, a persuasive argument. The more a person hears something, the more likely he or she is to begin to believe its validity. This is an area that many B2B companies underestimate. I often see marketers and salespeople get bored with the same messaging, to their own detriment. Remember that it takes seven to thirteen touches just to get a lead. Don't assume people remember everything your sales or marketing touch points said.

Familiarity bias: Politically correct or not, our brains favor members of our own social groups. This can go beyond ethnic and social groups, but here, again, when we see people familiar to us, our brains trust the provided information. Familiarity is one of the most common heuristics. Branding helps because it directs initial impressions *and* provides a long-term framework of recognition and trust. When you combine this with consistency and repetition, your brand offers the mental associations buyers will use to catalog their impressions of your company and your value.

Loss aversion: We respond more strongly to loss than to gain. Loss aversion implies that losses loom in our minds about twice as large as equivalent gains. It is significant for you to realize that your prospect will focus more on the risks than the rewards when making decisions.

Inertia: We tend to interpret information the same way over time and rely on familiar assumptions. Don't underestimate how difficult it is to change people's minds and preferences. This is especially important in positioning. If you find your business in a situation where you need to reposition your brand, you must first acknowledge buyers' perceptions and seek strategies that will help people shift their opinions, rather than try to convince them you are different from what they first thought. In branding, you must begin with what is true about you because your customers already have a preconceived notion of how to understand you. Simply saying you are different from what they assumed is not enough to make it so. It's critical to remember, also, that the data suggests the most common reason B2B companies don't close a deal is because the prospect decides not to move forward. If you are losing deals to the status quo, this is inertia at work.

Confirmation bias: We tend to favor and believe information that confirms what we already believe. This influences not only what we pay attention to but how we interpret information and even what and how we remember information. This reinforces why it is critical to begin your messaging choreography with mirroring how those of a certain buyer persona see their problem.

Social proof: When unsure how to proceed, we'll often look for cues as to how others make a decision. Reading reviews, recognizing prominent clients or endorsements, and using testimonials are all examples of social proof. When the social proof comes from people or companies who share your buyer personas, it's all the more powerful.

Contrast effect: When we compare options to one another, we tend to exaggerate our opinion of something more than if we had considered that same thing by itself. For example, you're more likely to be impressed by an average-looking person if that person is standing next to a less attractive person than if you had seen him or her alone. Pricing comparisons, stories that provide context, and before-and-afters are good examples.

Anchoring: Our exposure to a number—even a random number—will serve as a reference point against which we'll compare our options. Do not lead with a low number when verbally giving pricing options, as the buyer's brain will anchor to it.

Reciprocity: In general, humans don't like to feel indebted to anyone, and the desire to pay someone back can be powerful motivation. Have you ever bought something you didn't want or didn't like after accepting a free sample? This is the reciprocity heuristic in effect. Free guides, demos, and trials are great examples, and they can lead into other heuristics, such as familiarity. Be aware, however, that this heuristic has been overused in certain areas, so your generosity should be authentic and of high value. It's my philosophy to give what you want to receive but not expect a payoff. Do it because it's the right thing to do as a servant leader. If you follow the principles in this book, you will do this naturally.

This is by no means an exhaustive list—it's not even close. So why, you might ask, bring this up at all? To reinforce one simple message: we are not logical beings; we are emotional beings. Dry self-oriented marketing *does not work*. The science of decision-making heavily influences the strategies recommended in this book, so you'll be incorporating these heuristics already, but it helps to be aware of the additional reasons why this road map works.

If you want to get people's attention, you must talk to them about them. Use words, images, and emotions that they already prioritize to open the door to conscious recognition of your product or service. Tap into emotion over logic. Know what your buyer personas care about, and pay attention to and help your buyers by using this insight to get their attention. Seek simplicity in your messaging to avoid overload, and consider ways in which the thoughtful use of heuristics can make it a little easier for a prospect to choose you.

Dacia Coffey

The Buyer's Brain and Your Brand

Now it's time to talk about how you are perceived and what you must do to distill your truth into a clear, finite impression. It's time to talk about your brand. You just learned that existing associations that people have made in the past can predispose them toward one decision over another at the subconscious level. Branding is the art of aligning with and directing people's emotions and opinions on the conscious and subconscious levels. Your brand is not how you view your company; it's how outsiders view your company. A truly amazing brand sits at the intersection of its incomparable advantage and what its customers care about. Your brand should attract and appeal to your ideal customers, so if you're choosing your color palette and symbols based solely on your personal preferences, you could be in trouble.

There is a *ton* of material written about brand and branding—much of it, of course, from the B2C point of view. And much of what you read will only add to any confusion rather than reduce it. Thus, my goal for this chapter is twofold. First, I want to convince you of the absolutely critical, nonnegotiable importance of branding without writing a whole 'nother book on the topic. Secondly, I'd like to distill the conversation of branding into something practical and actionable for you to employ. Great brands don't get built or reinvented overnight, but you must be intentional about the process.

> The best time to plant a tree was twenty years ago.
> The second-best time to plant a tree is now.
> —Chinese proverb

Branding is science, art, messaging, culture, and customer experience wrapped into one communication strategy, and in the B2B world, it is wildly undervalued, which means it holds a world of opportunity. As buyers' choices get more complex, your actual message needs to become more human. Technology has bred a more intense need for a personal touch, and this makes branding more important than ever before in the B2B world. Your first impression is a lasting impression. Before you spend more money on promotion, make sure your core brand and message will impress and resonate. Your brand must have appeal and intentionally communicate to your target market to help them understand you and prefer you over your competition at the gut level.

The word *brand* or *branding* has at times become synonymous with marketing in general. It's true that your brand is overlaid against everything you do, but the semantics can get complicated, so I've organized this discussion around the practical application of brand principles. The American Marketing Association defines a *brand* as "a name, term, design, symbol, or any other feature that identifies one seller's goods or service as distinct from those of other sellers."[37] The International Organization for Standardization further explains that a brand assists in creating "distinctive images and associations in the minds of stakeholders, thereby generating economic benefit/values."[38] Thus, your brand is not just your logo and color scheme; it is instead what people believe about you when they engage with *anything* representing your organization.

> Branding is the art of aligning what you want people
> to think about your company with what people actually
> do think about your company. And vice versa.
> —Jay Baer

Branding is how you show up in the world. It's how people feel about you, so it's a never-ending, always-evolving aspect of marketing and competition. You can't rest on your laurels, because minds change, experiences change, and markets change. Your brand works for you or against you on the subconscious level because the brain processes vast amounts of data, with the primary source being visual information, which the brain processes and organizes in a fraction of a second. As the saying goes, seeing is believing. What visuals are you using to provide that critical first impression, and what emotional signals do your visual communications trigger? Does your branding have a polish that is appealing, or does it look homemade or old? Are you conveying professionalism and capability, or does your brand appear dated or mom-and-pop, suggesting that you're small, you don't innovate, or you don't keep up with the times? If you are in an industry with very strong brands, how are you standing out? Could those in the market consistently choose words that clearly name your position and corporate personality? If someone were to match your name to a competitor's logo, would it be ridiculous or not even noticeable?

The point I'm trying to make is that every single communication choice you make tells a story. Not making a choice (i.e., not investing in your brand) is still making a choice. Your lack of attention to this matter might communicate that you are apathetic or pay no attention to detail. Make no mistake: people will draw conclusions based on how you choose to communicate, and these conclusions are what they'll use to form their comparisons between you and your competition. No matter how diligently your salespeople prospect, hustle, and follow up, they are at a huge disadvantage if the brand doesn't communicate excellence when they aren't in the room.

The best doesn't always win; the best at removing fear does. Solid branding removes fear because it demonstrates intentionality, competence, and allure. As for myself, I prefer to be the master of my destiny and communicate strength rather than wait around for scraps or missed opportunities left over by my competition. Do yourself a favor and make it easy for the market to trust you. Stack the cards in your favor. The achievements of a great brand are as follows:

- awareness
- trust
- belief
- memorability
- desire
- reputation
- likability
- belonging
- loyalty
- consistency

So how do you build an amazing brand? I organize the elements of your brand into three groups: (1) brand strategy, (2) brand identity, and (3) brand experience. A lot of content written on branding bleeds into the distribution of your brand, but really, those are your customer-acquisition tactics. How, not where, you execute them is what matters when talking about brand.

Brand Strategy

Your brand strategy, of course, includes the external considerations of your strategy: buyer personas, positioning, and messaging choreography. It then connects those considerations to your purpose, promise, product, and personality, with the goal of generating a specific emotional reaction. The strategic elements direct and infuse your brand with direction and meaning. They are your decision-making criteria and include your

- buyer personas,
- positioning,
- messaging,
- purpose,
- promise,
- product,
- personality,
- company-product architecture (when necessary), and
- desired customer emotion.

We start with buyer personas and the messaging that will resonate so that you are making decisions with a clear idea of who will judge your communication choices and what message they will convey. Next, brand strategy considers the market reality—your positioning. Are you more or less expensive? Is your quality higher or lower? Is your service faster or slower? What type of culture does your company exude? It all starts with who you serve and where in the spectrum of options your offering lies. Your brand helps you claim a specific and consistent place in your buyers' minds. Your value and price have no significance to your buyers unless they know what to compare you to. Branding helps customers organize their options.

Walmart provides lower quality, lower pricing, and a lower level of customer service than Nordstrom. Does this make the company less effective or less successful in the market? Of course not. Walmart knows the people it seeks to serve, and those in the company make communication decisions in alignment with the best way to communicate accurately. As does Nordstrom. Each has chosen branding appropriate to its desired place in the market and seeks to execute on its brand promises consistently. Customers use the same indicators to determine market positioning in their B2B roles, just as they do as consumers.

From a marketing perspective, this is encapsulated in your differentiation strategy. One of my clients in the financial industry appropriately framed the company's predicament as "drowning in a sea of sameness" that defined that industry. I've adopted that "sea of sameness" phrase because it captures the heart of the problem. Crafting a powerful differentiation message does not mean "How do I communicate that we're better, faster, or cheaper?" Differentiation means "to be different." Different! Purple instead of blue. Small instead of big. Funny instead of serious. But truly desiring escape from the sea of sameness requires courage. You can't look at your competitors as context. You must dive into the space where you are incomparable. It's wise to consider three areas to help you stand out from the competition: (1) what makes your offering different, (2) how you do business, and (3) why you care.

Being the -*Est*

You can differentiate by having a *truly* superior product. Maybe you're the first to market, you disrupted a market, or your -*est* (e.g., fastest, cheapest, or best) is so superior that it's nearly impossible for your prospects to choose your competitor once they've heard of you.

For now. Eventually, a copycat or a different type of disrupter is going to come along and make your innovation obsolete. This is a never-ending game of cat and mouse, where your customer loyalty lasts only as long as your best features remain unique. It's important to remember that this does not refer to quality. This relates only to your offering's truly unique and superior features—ones that no one else can claim. The danger is that many companies are so in love with their superiority that they forget the "What's in it for me?" It doesn't matter whether you're better; it matters only whether your prospective customers think so *and* believe that being better matters to their desired outcome.

Magnifying Your You-ness

This is where your humanity and your story enter the picture. There is only one you. There is no other organization on the planet exactly like yours. No one else brings the exact combination of insight, point of view, people, culture, experience, opinion, passion, strengths, strategy, and every other characteristic that defines your organization. By default, you are *already* different. So now you need to own it: clarify your specialness, and be intentional about going bigger with your strengths. Simply put, this is how you do what you do.

For example, your operational, or process, excellence might result in efficiency, unique customization, delivery, delight, speed, or any number of things. Equally, the personality of your business can affect customer experience, ease of doing business with you, referrals, and reviews because the emotion of doing business with you is so positive. Or you may specialize in a specific market, problem, or product that not only helps speed up sales cycles and delivery because of your mastery but can help you justify a higher price, because research shows buyers will pay a premium for specialization. (Why? Because it removes fear and increases confidence.) No one else runs business in the exact manner you do, because no one else has your daily truth. The reality of how you are different lies in your stories. It's found in the vivid descriptions of *how* you go about your business and how this affects your customers. But just know that this aspect of differentiation is a difficult one to clarify, because everywhere you go, there you are. It's difficult to know *how* you're different because you are saturated in your own environment, assumptions, and day-to-day reality. This is where an outside consultant can be wildly beneficial.

Communicating Your Why

You may have seen the 2010 TED talk "How Great Leaders Inspire Action" by Simon Sinek. (If not, stop and go watch it now! I'll wait.) In the past decade, we've heard this time and again—so why is our *why* so underutilized? Because it's truly hard work, and it's work that takes time and has no finish line. Sure, you might eventually craft the right words for your mission and vision statement, but truthfully, the exact phrasing might need to be updated from time to time. More important, your why is not about the perfect copy but instead about doing business with real heart and putting people first in action, not just in word. This work takes a heavy dose of self-awareness, as well as dedication to infusing your entire organization with meaning. You must cast a vision of success that goes beyond the total of your invoices and reputation.

Because I believe so passionately in the importance of this, I'm going to do you a favor: I won't sugarcoat this. Once you've claimed your why, the implementation goes far beyond updating some words and talking about it at a sales meeting. Your message will change, of course, but if the commitment is there, a cascade of decisions and investments lie before you. Your bonus structures might need to change, your hiring and firing criteria will definitely need to change, and you'll need to be intentional about what it looks like to live out your why and your core values. Your entire approach to business should eventually be seen through the lens of your purpose and beliefs. But this is the work of legacy and impact and of building a business that changes people's lives—even if you're in IT, manufacturing, industrial distribution, finance, or any of the other complicated, behind-the-scenes companies that make this world go around.

I do a lot of speaking and writing on using your work to bless the world, and I don't have enough space in this book to tackle what it takes to find and communicate your why here. But there are many resources, including my company's very popular list of the best examples of mission and vision statements, which has a DIY workbook to get you started. You can find it at https://www.themarketingblender.com/vision-mission-statements/.

Your why statement is critical because it allows your prospects and customers to find common ground with you. When you have clearly identified your why, it will shine through your communication and even your stories. The alignment your prospects register might be related to values they share with you, similar or shared histories, or possibly a shared vision for the future. Whatever the parallel, your purpose helps you communicate that you are trustworthy because you are similar.

If you're somewhere in the middle of your organization, don't lose heart, and don't ignore this work. Small divisions and teams can have why statements and be mission oriented inside larger organizations. But for a why to have a *marketable* impact on the success of a business, this work must come from the top down. It cannot be delegated. Be brave enough to dive into the personal work needed for this. Get a consultant to help you see your blind spots and hear the themes you take for granted. Do the work. You'll find your joy, and the market will respond.

Your Archetype and Your Customer's Emotion

All this work culminates in people's emotional response to your organization. Why so much attention to emotion? you might be asking. Remember—decision-making happens in the limbic system of the brain, which controls emotion. It controls neither logic nor communication. Let me repeat this: decision-making happens at emotional ground zero. We went through how to build your incomparable advantage in chapter 5 because we often overcomplicate our words and sink into logic and argument to feel comfortable. I have found that we need to get the words organized and out of the way in order for us to do the critical work of branding because logical words don't help in branding. Your brand sets the emotional stage for your success.

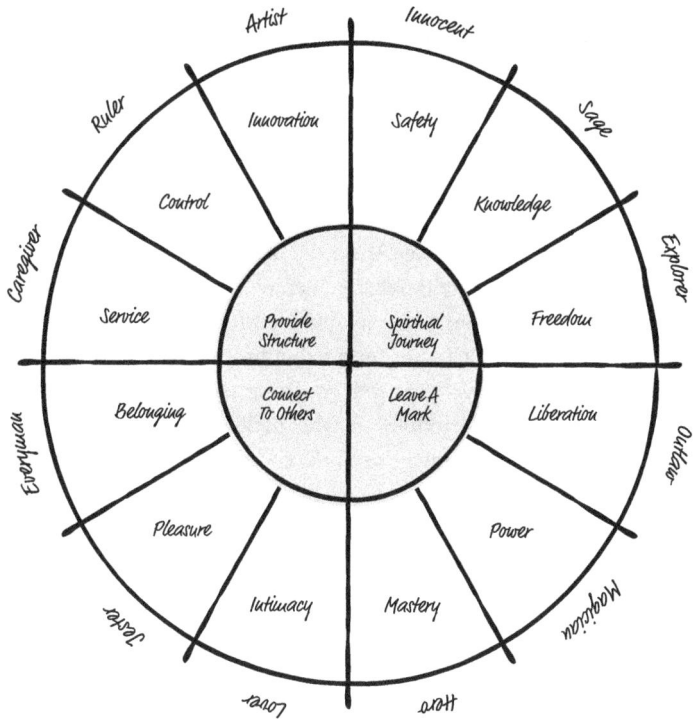

This is once again a great place to employ a framework for understanding your incomparable advantage in emotion and relationship. As people, we understand ourselves within the social roles we play in our lives, and we have immediate context around what different roles represent. So it's helpful to look at your company as a character with a distinct, recognizable personality. You'll be amazed at how effective this can be. Who are you to your customers when delivering on your strengths? Your role is called your *archetype*. Archetypes are the most common characters found in stories that represent our relationships with one another. Carl Jung popularized their use in psychology for understanding personalities. In literature and screen writing, they help readers quickly empathize with characters because their personalities are familiar and believable stereotypes. They are highly recognizable and tap into our universal human emotions, experiences, and ways of relating to others. As such, archetypes lend both a symbolic and a familiar magnetism to brands.

Looking at how customers experience your organization as if it's a character in a movie can be poignant and massively effective in helping you distill down the essence of who you are in the marketplace. To employ an archetypical structure for your brand, identify which role your company plays in its customer interactions. Taking a look at the graphic, you'll see the circle is divided into twelve roles and subdivided into four quadrants. Each quadrant (and the three roles within it) is organized around the universal transformation that you achieve for your customer and even the world, at the center of the circle. Additionally, on the outside of the circle, you'll see phrases that relate to what you enjoy and aspire to culturally.

It's critical to start with the quadrant and not the name of the role because all people will have preconceived notions about who they believe themselves to be individually, as well as strong negative associations with different roles. These gut reactions are what make archetypes so profoundly effective, but they can sabotage the work of identifying the real archetype that your organization embodies culturally. Additionally, there are no good or bad archetypes. Just like human beings, each one brings strengths and, conversely, an Achilles' heel. Your best customers already subconsciously know which archetype you are; you cannot pick an archetype simply because that's what you want to be. Your brand already exists, and it's your job to align with your current reality and maximize the best aspects of your role.

If you look at the previous strategic components, which quadrant best aligns with the transformation you create for customers shown on the inside of the circle? Does it also align with the culture and mission of your organization (i.e., the outside descriptions)?

Once you've narrowed down the quadrant, move to the two middle layers: (1) the output and (2) the archetypes themselves. These output words describe what you deliver to your customers. So if the inner part of the circle is the transformation you provide, then the output is how you enable that transformation. What is the final culmination of your value?

Quadrant (1) (the top left corner) commonly focuses on the benefit to the individuals in an organization, (2) is related to external significance and influence in the world, (3) impacts the relationships among stakeholders, and (4) often helps your clients maximize how they serve or engage their customers. To home in on your core archetype, gather more detailed information on each one at themarketingblender.com/brand-archetypes. You can also see great examples of corporate archetypes in today's business world.

Don't be surprised or alarmed if you believe you fit two archetypes in different quadrants. If it turns out they are both applicable, you'll have to make a decision about which one is primary. This is critical. So many B2B companies don't want to draw a line in the sand, because they want to throw everything they've got at everyone they could possibly serve, but this is simply poor decision-making and a lack of strategic discipline. Most leaders know that being decisive is critical for success; there are numerous ways to solve problems, but at the end of the day, you must pick one. As leaders, we're all comfortable with this in hiring, operational improvements, and financial decisions. But in marketing, many of us are not willing to draw the line in the sand, and it waters down our potency in the market.

Let me give you an example of making a decision. In my marketing agency, we transform customers' marketing and sales efforts by implementing and optimizing marketing strategies, marketing plans, branding, and digital marketing. Through this process, their business development goes from haphazard to highly structured. More specifically, I'm known for my energy and innovation, which of course influences the type of team members my firm attracts. They in turn deliver highly alluring creations. Thus, our brand is based on the artist archetype. However, we are also very much the sage archetype. We are passionate about being guides and educating our clients and the market at large. On a one-to-one level, we play a mentor or counselor role, helping people realize their potential in themselves rather than just doing the work for them. The sage archetype influences our processes and ways of working, but we decided to lead with the artist in our symbolic representation of what we do, because while we allow ourselves to make individual impact, the final output we create is organizational growth and competitive advantage for our clients.

If the founder still runs your company, it is extremely likely that the organizational archetype will embody the founder's primary archetype. This is not bad; it's just oftentimes true. It's better to name and strengthen your organizational personality rather than constantly argue the point, staying mired in fruitless frustration. If you truly get stuck in identifying which lead archetype you should choose, go back to your buyer personas, and ask yourself which one resonates the most with them and which role you end up playing with your best customers.

Brand Identity

Once you outline the brand strategy, it's time to bring in the creative elements that will foster that immediate recognition, allure, and consistency you desire. Your brand identity includes the visual components, style, voice, and guidelines that contribute to the consistency critical to your brand equity, which results in economic benefit for your company. While there is a wide range of elements that compose your brand identity (based on how large your organization is), the core elements include your

- name;
- logo;
- colors;
- visuals and symbols;
- imagery;
- fonts;
- style;
- brand voice;
- tagline, if applicable; and
- brand guidelines on how the elements are to be used together.

These elements then need to be applied consistently to your communication tools with special care given to your website, sales collateral and presentation materials, and signage. You must make communication decisions that convey your personality, appeal to your buyer personas, and stir the emotion that helps your prospects better understand and trust you.

The creative aspect of your brand is more critical than it's ever been. Research shows that the brain appreciates beauty. Beauty holds our attention and invokes curiosity and indulgence. We slow down for beauty. In an age of too little time and too little attention, that's currency you can't afford to ignore. Subconsciously, we equate beauty with value, desirability, art, power, and stature. According to Maslow's hierarchy of needs, only once basic survival needs are met can we afford to make more spiritual and preferential decisions. Beauty speaks to all, but it becomes apparent only when we allow ourselves to perceive it. When your website and other touch points are beautiful, you're giving customers and prospects a more meaningful and enjoyable experience. You are taking them up the value chain. And when people like what they see, they stay longer. Engage the senses intentionally in all your touchpoints. While the sight is the primary conveyance of the brand, it's not the only one, which is why the brand strategy work is so critical. When you choose your brand elements, your brand strategy becomes your decision-making criteria, not your personal preferences. Names, words, and sounds have connotations. Are you thinking through what those might be for your buyer personas? Colors have strong emotional correlations. Are you choosing colors that align with the emotional response you want to evoke?

YELLOW - OPTIMISM / CLARITY / WARMTH

ORANGE - FRIENDLY / CHEERFUL / CONFIDENCE

RED - EXCITEMENT / YOUTHFUL / BOLD

PURPLE - CREATIVE / IMAGINATIVE / WISE

BLUE - TRUST / DEPENDABLE / STRENGTH

GREEN - PEACEFUL / GROWTH / HEALTH

GREY - BALANCE / NEUTRAL / CALM

The same holds true for shapes. The associations, however, differ from culture to culture. You must know your buyer personas to be able to navigate these decisions.

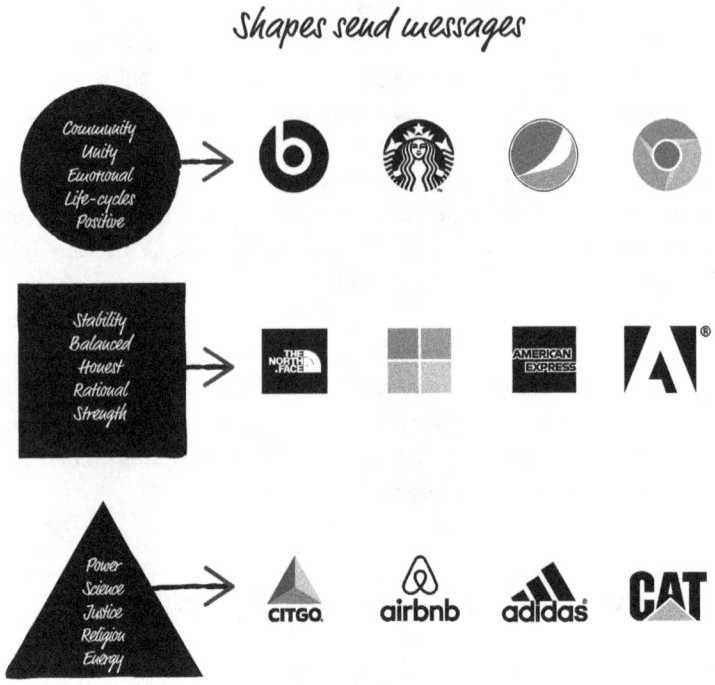

Brand Experience

The third group involves how your brand is distributed through your employees, operations, and customer service. I refer to this as the *brand experience*. Oftentimes, you'll hear about customer experience (especially as it relates to customer service); experiential marketing (which often relates to live events or activations); or even user experience (commonly referred to as UX and related to the customers of your product interface, digital marketing, and other functional touchpoints). This is truly where the rubber meets the road, because your strategy, brand promise, purpose, values, and brand identity all culminate in real human interactions. In short, do your employees actually live the commitments and strategic decisions that you've made and, more important, that your customers expect from your brand?

> Perceptions are verbs.
> —Jean-Marie Dru

It does not matter how beautiful, innovative, or clever your branding is; if your marketing experience creates frustration (also known as *friction*), or, worse, if it sucks to do business with you, no design, copy, or mission statement in the world can save you. Your brand at the end of the day *is* your truth because perception is reality.

In the short term, good branding stacks the deck in your favor, while poor branding diminishes your perceived value. Great branding maximizes the effectiveness of all your promotional efforts to garner greater returns. Vigilant, honest, and meaningful branding—in other words, *excellent* branding—gives you a competitive advantage and increases the value of your business. Maybe we should call branding your *customer strategy*.

In the long term, It's the only marketing tool related to profit. An established and successful brand can help you develop a more profitable pricing strategy and increase your company's valuation. But it takes purposeful, consistent, and deliberate commitment to building a customer experience that is so good it ends up being symbolized within the colors, shapes, and phrases you've chosen for your logo and name. In a world where the speed of change is accelerating exponentially, it's no wonder that people respond to consistency and brands that can be counted on.

Employment Branding

I would be remiss if I didn't address one final, but critical, point about the application and importance of your brand. It's not only your prospects who are taking cues from your brand communication to make decisions about you.

It's also your future employees. World-class organizations attract world-class talent—not only the best and the brightest but the personalities and the values that will be a cultural fit. When you effectively communicate the truth of your organization, your prospective employees will recognize your organization as a place where they will (or won't) thrive and grow.

We have seen a growing gap in skills alignment, as well as phases in which there have been more jobs than workers. The competition for great people is more intense than ever. Your brand is the edge you need in order to attract the people who will protect your culture and take your company to the next level.

If your brand isn't everything I've described in this chapter, I do have to ask you, Why not? Believe me—you can't afford to let this slide.

The Rearview Mirror

- Decision-making is not logical but emotional.
- The brain is a highly efficient filter and prioritizes only the stimuli that already have meaning to us.
- Because of the vast amount of information the brain filters and the large number of daily decisions it makes, the brain employs heuristics, or mental shortcuts, to reduce the cognitive load of complex decisions. These heuristics align with the strategic recommendations of this book.
- Knowing the science behind decision-making further helps us to be customer centric and to maximize our effectiveness.
- Branding makes you recognizable in the market, which can increase your organization's bottom line, but it is based on your prospects' actual perceptions versus how you want to be perceived.
- Branding can be broken down into three segments: (1) brand strategy, (2) brand identity, and (3) brand experience. You then apply your decisions from these three categories to all your customer-acquisition tactics.
- Add resonance and impact to your brand messaging with a multitiered approach to your differentiation strategy, combining what is great about your offering, how you deliver in a unique way, and why you care.
- Archetypes provide a powerful framework for making clear brand decisions that will draw the right emotional response from your buyer personas.
- Your branding must culminate in your customer's experience.
- Branding must also be applied to attract the right talent.

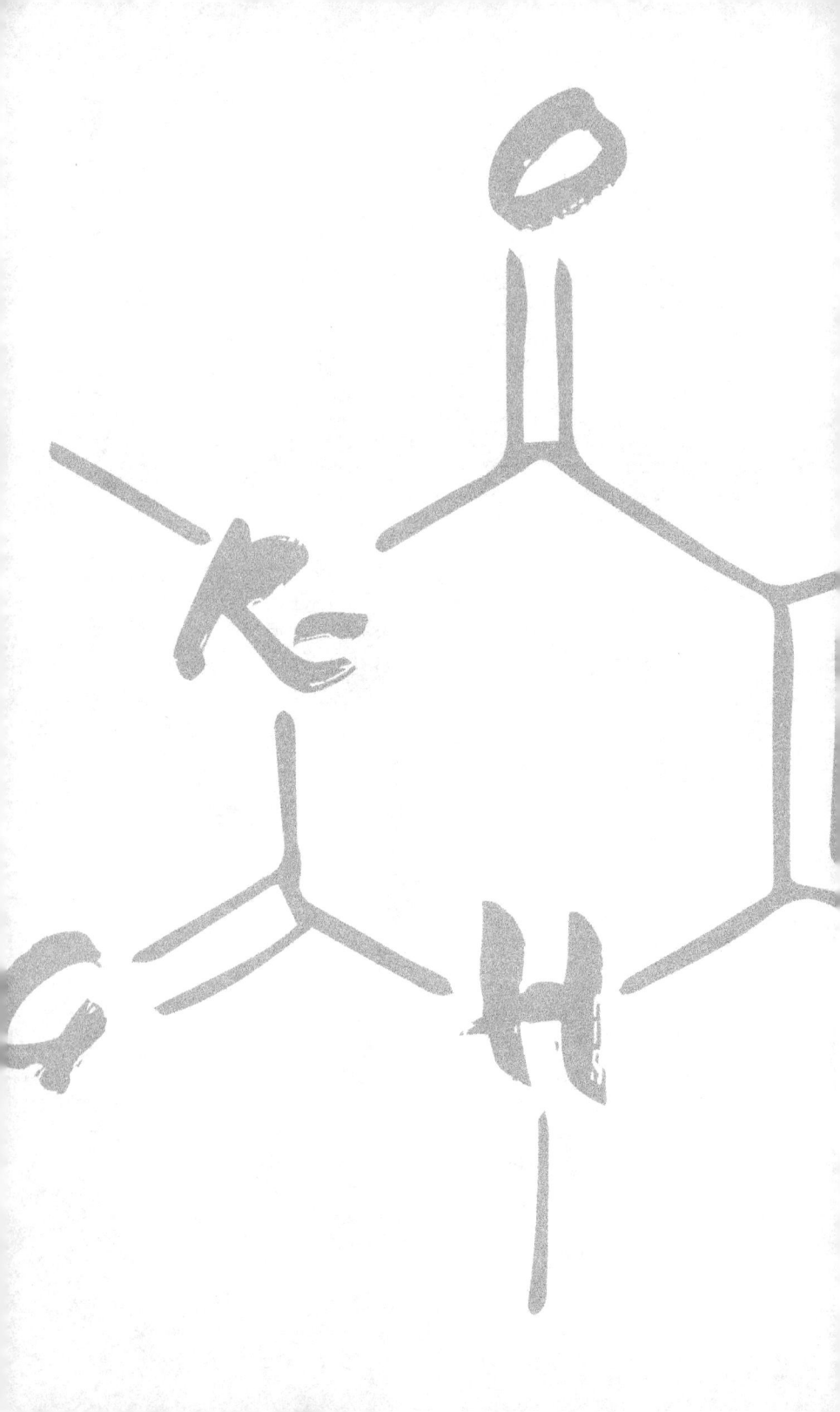

7
EXECUTION AND ROI

It's time to tie it all together in your execution, and the key is to build with the end in mind. The work leading up to this created your strategic foundation. Now it's time to organize your launch workflow and measure the effectiveness of your efforts. It's important that you not get lost in tactical details but instead structure your execution in a way that maintains strategic integrity. Having a consistent approach will help everyone stay on the same page and align on the topic of ROI.

Historically, a marketer's performance is gauged through marketing metrics, which focus on tactics, instead of financial metrics, which focus on impact. To understand impact and make the best decisions regarding revenue growth, you must align marketing success with the financial language of the business. With the right framework, you can see where you biggest problems lie, prioritize their solutions to drive both short-term and long-term growth, and execute your plans with finesse.

> Vision without execution is hallucination.
> —Thomas Edison

With your strategic elements in place, you must now masterfully execute your marketing. So where do you begin? With the end in mind, of course, which requires a shift in how you're looking at your marketing plan. Your marketing plan from chapter 4 is structured to support the buyer's journey. It's tempting to want to build out campaigns and headlines to get people's attention first, but what happens when it works? You'll have people curious and interested, but you won't have anything in place to convert their interest into inquiry. Talk about wasted money and opportunity that you can't get back. Instead, I believe outstanding execution follows an ABC framework:

> Align your message and brand with your strategic plan and goals.

> Build the brand collateral, campaigns, and calls to action to convert interest into inquiry to help prospects more efficiently proceed through their decision-making process.

> Champion your message and confidently invest in promotion knowing that you have mapped out the prospect's experience of interacting with your marketing.

If your brand and messaging cannot convert interest into inquiry, it doesn't matter how brilliant or wide reaching your promotion is. You must start with the assets, where your messaging and branding convert interest into inquiry and inquiry into sales. Once you have stacked these cards in your favor, then it's time to distribute your message to the masses.

Converting Interest to Inquiry

We've talked a considerable amount about how both the buyer and the seller progress through the decision-making process, but a huge bottleneck in the buyer's journey happens when the next step isn't clear. *Calls to action*, or CTAs, provide cues to potential buyers about what they need in order to proceed. CTAs are what you suggest to your buyer personas to assist them in solving their problem or achieving their goal. One of the most common mistakes I see in B2B marketing is the neglect or misuse of CTAs. Often, there simply won't be a clear CTA in the collateral, trade show booth, ad, or web page. And when there is a CTA, it's almost always "Contact us." This is like asking someone to marry you on the first date. It reeks of desperation, and it rarely works.

In chapter 4, we discussed the three exchanges: (1) attention, (2) time, and (3) money. Your CTAs align with the exchanges, providing progress for the buyer and communicating where the prospect is in the buyer's journey. Think of your CTA as an ATM. There is an exchange for attention, time, or money based on the value a prospect can withdraw from you.

In the attention exchange, your ask is something that can be accomplished quickly and requires little to no commitment. Examples include watching a video, visiting a specific landing page through an ad or post, clicking a second page on a website, hovering one's phone over an ad, or following on social media. One additional CTA is implicit: you're asking people to *remember* you. This is why B2C companies use mnemonic devices like rhymes, mascots, celebrities, and endless amounts of repetition. These are best practices underutilized in the B2B world.

CTAs in the time exchange might include attending a webinar or event; downloading a guide, checklist, or other resource; subscribing to a channel, podcast, or email series; and taking the free assessment. These tools help to educate prospects.

As prospects move in to close the deal, where they know they are going to make a purchase, the marketing CTAs include things like contacting the company, scheduling a free consultation, getting a quote, and setting up a demo.

While this sounds simple, many B2B marketers don't have great CTAs because their creation requires a lot of time and attention from subject-matter experts. Guides, checklists, videos, white papers, articles, and any other high-value content require input from the operations team. Most B2B organizations don't prioritize this because they don't see marketing as a customer-focused activity, and the projects wither on the vine. But if you truly desire an aligned organization that lives

> Setting up a demo is often put too early in the sales process because organizations view this as the crossover to a sale and rush toward the demo. In actuality, it represents a high level of commitment for the customer. When this CTA is placed too early in the process, it can delay progress because the prospect does not have enough information yet, or it can lead to a scenario in which multiple demos must be given.

your mission every day, servant leadership in your business-development communication is critical, and a cross-functional team must give attention to these activities.

If you are not getting the results you want from your marketing, take a close look at what value you are offering to prospects before they buy from you. If your value is given only after an invoice, it becomes incredibly difficult in this busy, fast, and competitive world to convince people to invest their time and attention in you unless they have referrals from existing customers.

Once you have your marketing strategy, plan, messaging, and branding in place, review the sales map and consider what the prospect wants and needs in order to proceed. What questions does your prospect ask? What and where are common misunderstandings inherent in the prospect's choices? What immediate insight can you provide that leads to your differentiator? Prioritize your topics using these types of questions. Your CTAs provide the progress that will help both you and your buyer personas progress through the decision-making process openly and respectfully.

Prioritizing Tactics and Measuring Effectiveness

No conversation about execution is complete without a discussion on budgeting, prioritization, and outcomes. Extending the philosophy of structuring your execution with the end in mind, you must identify the tactics that will have the biggest impact on your business now and that you can build on to create sustainable success in the future. No one has unlimited resources, so you must get bang for your business-development buck. Budgeting and ROI are two sides of the same coin. You must make informed decisions about where to put your money, time, and attention, and then you must measure the effectiveness of those tactics to find areas of improvement or redirection. Both budgeting and measuring the return on your marketing investment are challenging conversations at best, and at worst, they are hotbeds for internal misalignment, shortsighted planning, and a lot of frustration. I'm neither an analyst nor a math whiz, so this is not going to be a deep dive into algorithms, weighted averages, marketing analytics, or investment calculations. Instead, we're going to take a holistic and practical look at how to understand ROI, how to allocate budget, and how to create agreement within your organization about how ROI is measured so you can then maximize your results.

The language of business can be boiled down to a few critical numbers: revenue, expenses, profit, cash flow, and equity. In business, we pull different levers to impact these numbers. To improve cash flow, the finance department pulls levers such as adjusting terms, managing credit, and getting aggressive on collections. To impact profit, companies will cut costs or increase pricing. If they want revenue growth, companies generally must pull a marketing or sales lever, so it's not healthy to refer to marketing as a cost center when it is the lifeblood of the organization. In the same vein, it is not acceptable for marketing to rely solely on metrics that do not clearly communicate correlation to financial impact. Thus, it's critical to create an aligned understanding and language for marketing ROI.

To start, let's go ahead and look at some examples of marketing ROI calculations and why these haven't helped most organizations resolve this problem.

$$(\text{Your Sales Growth} - \text{Your Marketing Costs}) \div \text{Marketing Cost}$$

This simple approach sounds great, but what impact do market trends have on growth? Even if there are no positive market trends assisting with your revenue increase, this calculation assumes that your marketing costs are solely responsible for growth.

$$(\text{Your Sales Growth} - \text{Organic Sales Growth} - \text{Your Marketing Costs}) \div \text{Marketing Cost}$$

Neither of the preceding formulas acknowledges that many marketing campaigns are not designed to impact *today's* sales. A healthy marketing mix accounts for immediate revenue impact but also your pipeline for tomorrow's sales, as well as your long-term visibility and positioning with future decision makers.

Here's another option:

$$(\text{Customer Lifetime Value} - \text{Marketing Investment}) \div \text{Marketing Investment}$$

I really like this one and think it's incredibly important. However, there is no separation between the impact of the sales team and the impact of your marketing spend.

As you know by now, I advocate for sales and marketing to function as a unified team, so their figures shouldn't be broken out separately. However, the sales team is almost always given the credit for sales growth, which negates the role of marketing in the sales team's ability to close more deals.

There are numerous other calculations, especially for campaign effectiveness. Here's an example:

$$[((\text{Number of Leads} \times \text{Lead-to-Customer Rate} \times \text{Average Sales Price}) - \text{Cost of Ad Spend}) \div \text{Cost or Ad Spend}] \times 100$$

But how about the impact of the marketers themselves and their salaries? You see, each calculation comes with its own complexities and imperfections. Because it's a complicated environment both emotionally and financially, we need a new way to look at ROI that gives leadership decision-making insight into the effectiveness of their marketing *and* unifies the business-development approach to maximize revenue growth.

Marketers and leadership teams have a responsibility to build a bridge between the two languages of marketing metrics and financial performance. What I want to give you is a down and dirty way to understand marketing analytics and, more important, how to translate them into financial terms. It is time for marketing teams to learn how to speak the language of business: financial metrics. And it is time for the C-suite to stop being legalistic—and at times argumentative—in trying to drive a direct correlation between, say, a single social media post and its direct impact on revenue. It's time to view business development as a system you can optimize, much like how you optimize operational processes. Thus, you can then prioritize optimization efforts by finding and minimizing areas of waste, slowdowns, and lost opportunities within the total pipeline. So how do you do this? Let's begin with a visualization of the different types of customer outcomes that marketing can drive to move a prospect closer to a deal. We'll take a look at how marketing works using a funnel graphic.

You'll remember from chapter 4 that the buyer's journey goes from awareness to consideration to decision—and possibly to referral and more purchases. What can we measure in the buyer's journey?

Generate Interest: Awareness

First, your market must know you exist and what problem you solve. This is visibility. You cannot get leads if you are invisible. Visibility is the most financially expensive outcome to achieve and the hardest to measure. Examples of visibility metrics include impressions, audience size (if you speak from a stage), search engine optimization, and share of voice.

Next, you want your visibility to drive curiosity, and you want your prospects to act on that curiosity. This is measured by traffic. It means that people have heard of you and are spending a few seconds or minutes to intentionally check you out and, hopefully, cement your existence into their mental library of resources. Traffic can be measured on the trade show floor or by visitors to your websites, visitors to your landing pages, video views, and so forth. This measurement reflects how many people are researching you. You can also consider the quality of the traffic, chiefly by paying attention to how much time they are spending with you—for example, the amount of time they spend browsing your website or watching your videos.

Build Trust: Consideration

From traffic you created, how many prospects took an action and began to invest time into better understanding your expertise or your offering? We call these *conversions* because these movements show that you converted interest into action. People are now beginning to invest time in you.

There are different types of conversions, and they generally fall into one of two camps. One action involves prospects researching a need, resulting in their signing up for webinars, downloading pieces of content, or taking any actions where they spend time with you and possibly give you their email addresses. These are called *marketing-qualified leads*, or MQLs, because all you know about them is that they found your content or offer valuable or interesting. You haven't confirmed whether they are in your target market, or, if they are, whether they have the authority, real need, or budget to make a purchase. They are simply in your database now. Conversions can begin early in the buyer's journey and build on one another to nurture your prospect's understanding of their problem and interest in your ability to solve that problem. The two primary metrics for MQLs are (1) how large your email list is growing from your content marketing efforts and (2) how your lead scoring reflects the nurturing efforts (if you are using automation software). It's up to you to nurture these MQLs and validate their viability as potential customers through the additional actions they take.

When the MQLs trigger a conversation with a salesperson, who then validates that they are able and interested in a purchase, they become *sales-qualified leads*, or SQLs. SQLs are the next level of measurement. Out of the MQLs generated from your marketing efforts designed to request time and build trust with prospects, how many of them did turn into qualified opportunities?

Close the Deal: Decision

And, of course, we want as many SQLs as possible to become customers. Many companies prioritize closing ratios, but remember that your closing ratio and thus your revenue are lagging indicators. There is nothing you can do to impact this directly, because the activities leading up to it are in the past.

Viewing your total business-development pipeline, not just your sales-qualified pipeline, is the key to understanding marketing ROI. Once you set a baseline for where you stand in each of these action areas and with each of your buyer personas, then your goal becomes keeping as many people inside the funnel as possible. It also gives you a broad look at the impact your marketing may have in the future. If you invest heavily in visibility and traffic, it takes time for the investment to funnel through the rest of the buyer's journey, but it will help your sales in the future. Alternatively, if you're underinvesting in visibility, you could be creating future harm to your lead generation in the coming years and with future decision makers.

There is an attrition ratio from each level, with the goal being to maximize the ratios and cut waste and lost prospects. With this paradigm, you can numerically identify where your biggest business-development problems lie and prioritize your time, attention, and money to fixing these critical areas first and creating a continuous-improvement approach.

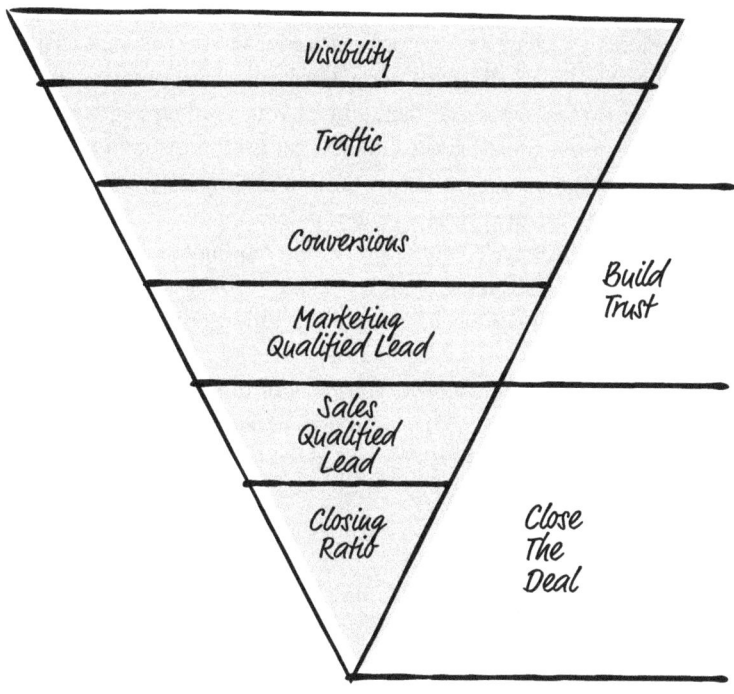

How to Improve Your Revenue Ratios

Once you have identified the key metrics for each level of your funnel, take a look at each ratio with a wide lens.

First, where are people falling out of your pipeline? Examine what the prospect experience is and where you can improve. Also, you'll want to take a look at the quality of each metric. You might have extremely high visibility and traffic but almost no conversions. It's very possible that you're in front of the wrong people. I'll give you an example. One of my company's clients manufactures storm-drain solutions. However, if you do a quick Google search for "storm drainage," you'll get a long list of products for backyard pools and home-improvement needs—but our client serves only the commercial market. It would do no good show up on page 1 of Google for any of these keyword terms because the percentage of this traffic would be useless.

Let's look at the scenario one level down in the funnel. What happens if you know that you're visible to the right people and that you have good traffic levels but you don't have enough conversions? Now you must examine the quality of your marketing execution. Look at and test your visuals, your message, your offer, the visual hierarchy of your landing pages, and the details of the prospect experience. The process continues down the funnel as new areas of opportunity arise in a continuous-improvement cycle. You can improve your nurture processes and your lead-qualification process, cut waste from your sales cycle, and improve your closing techniques.

This helps you understand organizationally if you're solving the correct problem. A lot of waste occurs because of misallocation of business-development money.

From a budgeting perspective, you can look at how you are allocating funds within this framework. It's not unlike how you maximize efficiency in operations. You look for bottlenecks and waste and then prioritize their solutions. The exact same principles apply to marketing.

Know Where Your Growth Will Come From

You need to create clarity for your business-development team members on the assumptions of how growth will occur. Unless you are a start-up, you'll likely have a percentage of your gross revenue associated with existing clients. You should clearly articulate your assumptions or goals about keeping clients and expanding your ability to serve them. Depending on your business model, this can be further broken down into products, divisions, or different types of engagements. Each should have its own number, and those numbers should assist you in breaking down the strategies and tactics you employ to achieve those numbers.

You'll also have a net-new revenue goal. Look at your closing ratios and conversion ratios to set assumptions about how many MQLs you need to keep your pipeline full. Depending on your business model and the size of your company, you can also make assumptions about how many leads come from each of your strategic initiatives and benchmark against those goals or assumptions. For example, if a predictable number of leads come in through speaking engagements, a specific number through paid digital advertising, and a certain number through referrals, you should think through and measure the ways in which you nurture and qualify the people who are engaging with your marketing to ensure your efforts lead to a sales conversation.

You'll also want to identify the areas of your sales process that you could improve to accelerate sales cycles or enhance closing ratios. Documenting your revenue assumptions can give you new perspective on the tactics you've chosen and where to focus your efforts and resources.

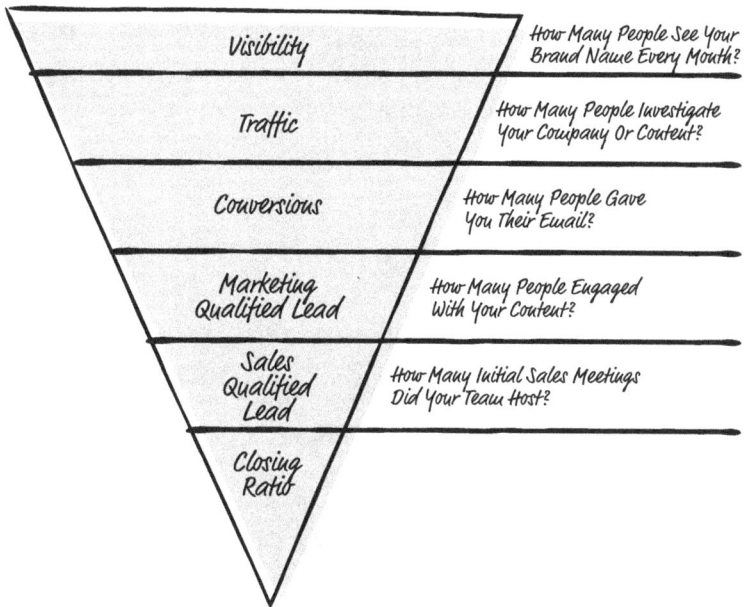

Alignment: Defining Success and Knowing the Pathway to Success

Using the revenue-ratio framework aligns your marketing and sales efforts into a unified point of view and helps with both check-ins and buy-ins. As you measure or check in on the efficacy of your marketing efforts, you can avoid getting lost in the weeds of individual tactics and instead view the health of your overall business-development system. Once you identify a problem, you can delegate the diagnosis and prescription to the correct people and hold them accountable for system improvement. This can assist with your team's buy-in on the strategy and bolster teamwork to achieve system improvement. We discussed that branding impacts profit, but marketing can impact profit in other ways as well. For example, a 2 percent reduction in client churn can equal a 10 percent reduction in expenses. Most customers are lost not because of problems but because of indifference. This is the perfect place for marketing to cross-functionally assist in plugging a gap in your growth.

Marketing is loaded with nuance and complexity because marketing is the business of connecting with humans—and humans are loaded with nuance and complexity. Of course, the ROI conversation is going to be nuanced and complex. But by agreeing on a big-picture framework for how marketing can impact the full engagement journey, you can clarify where your real problems and opportunities lie and make decisions (e.g., increase a marketing budget) in confidence.

The Rearview Mirror

- Build your execution plan by starting with the end in mind.
- The ABC framework—align, build, and champion—helps you convert interest into inquiry and set a path toward a sale.
- Begin by identifying your calls to action, or CTAs, for each of the exchanges in the sales cycle.
- A revenue-ratio framework can help you employ a holistic point of view on your marketing ROI to create agreement within your organization to maximize your results.
- Identify where you are losing prospects in your overall business-development system so you can prioritize and allocate budget effectively, eliminating waste, slowdowns, and lost opportunities within the total pipeline.
- Break down your revenue goals between current customers and net-new customers to further streamline your ability to create the most optimized pathway to a sale.
- By agreeing on a big-picture framework for how marketing can impact the full engagement journey, you can make confident decisions in sales and marketing based on the assumptions you can measure in achieving your revenue goals.

ENCOURAGEMENT

We have covered a lot of ground in this book. If you are feeling overwhelmed, don't throw in the towel. This is meaningful work with exponential payoff. When it comes to finding your organizational potential, it is always a journey based on progress, not perfection. Revenue growth can bring out hope, excitement, frustration, innovation, and personal growth. Growth includes inevitable change. The stakes are high, and there is no Pause button.

This is exactly why the effort to align sales and marketing—to create an environment of learning and continuous improvement—is crucial. Overreliance on your sales team's efforts is inappropriate in this digital age because you'll never reach your target market at scale. You'll inevitably hit a plateau based on the hours in the day and your ability to attract and train those so-called superstars who will likely leave in less than five years. And 2020 taught us how a "black swan" event can catch all of us off guard. At my company, The Marketing Blender, too many of our new clients in 2020 and 2021 came to us because they'd relied solely on trade shows, enthusiasm, existing relationships, and face-to-face selling. The definition of *good* is a moving target, and a healthy marketing mix with an aggressive review of effectiveness is the key way to remain agile as the speed of change accelerates.

Business development has no finish line since revenue is the lifeblood of your company. Nothing happens without a sale. The market and buyers' needs and behaviors constantly shift in a complex and dynamic way—that is simply the truth of human beings. We change, and thus, how we engage with one another must change. Alignment ensures your total business-development approach puts those you serve at the center of your outreach. After all, the real work of business development is helping another human solve a cumbersome problem. This is worthy and honorable, so our outreach should be too. Too much of today's professional communication is soul stealing. It's boring, bland, and wordy. We have only this one life to live; I'd prefer for my life and work to be as thought provoking and emotionally aligned as possible. I know you want the same. If you want great clients and great people, you must build a business-development approach that breeds excitement and collaboration while setting clear expectations that lead to a win for everyone. Quality people are attracted to quality organizations. Be the real deal, because success is slippery. Our work is of no use if we increase traffic but not leads, leads but not sales, sales but not profit, profit but not cash flow, or cash flow without enjoyment or lasting meaning. Your sales and marketing efforts should catalyze action in people so they can solve their problems and achieve their goals. What an exciting endeavor! Embrace a servant-leadership point of view where your team members feel empowered and excited to stir an emotional response from your ideal customers.

Encourage your people to improve by asking the right questions instead of constantly searching for a single magic talisman that will rescue lead generation and solve all your business-development problems. Tactics drive results only because of the strategy behind the execution. And as a leader, go ahead and ask about the definitions of words, test their assumptions, workshop your team's ideas of success, and communicate the why behind your questions and inquiries. An aligned sales and marketing framework challenges you as a leader to ditch the blame and avoid any defensive postures in your culture. This cover-your-ass mentality should not be the normal way of working. Refuse to accept this norm. Be brave and help your team do inspiring work.

Let's kill apathy in the B2B world by refusing to rush through our corporate communications and instead insist on serving and delighting people. Let's stop simply working for the weekend, because we will never have bold, fulfilling, and joyful lives if we don't harness our work for the greater good and allow our best selves to shine in our work habits. Be thoughtful with your words and your decisions. Great communication makes things so, but great communication takes preparation and intentionality. You deserve to live your best life. Great organizations deserve to grow. Your current and future customers deserve outstanding delivery. It is worthy to desire growth beyond your current state. Real ROI begins and ends with unity and clear communication around success.

I believe that we all have spiritual fingerprints. Just as no two people on the planet have the same pattern on their hands, no two people in the history of the world—past, present, or future—have the same experiences, upbringing, gifts, talents, strengths, training, personality, style, and background as you. Remember we are all incomparable. There is no comparison because you are the only you that will ever exist. And this is the truth of every organization as well. The spiritual fingerprint of your organization has the power to create powerful transformation in the world. When your organization aligns around common frameworks, goals, and values, opportunities open up for you to have greater impact. You can and should create impact beyond just those who receive invoices from you. This is good for the world and for your bottom line because your actions and intentions will attract the best people, the best opportunities, and the best individual output, which can result in a lifetime of happy customers. It is in your hands to build an organization that has the eyes to see a bigger future.

I envision a business world full of meaning, connection, and prosperity for all of us—but it will take all of us to make this a reality.

Go big.
Care more.
Be awesome.

Onward and upward!
Dacia

RESOURCES FOR YOUR TEAM

Workbook and resources: DaciaCoffey.com.

For real-world tips and examples, subscribe to the *Corporate Caffeine* podcast on your favorite platform.

Interested in training for your team or attending one of our training sessions? Visit DaciaCoffey.com.

For more information on having Dacia speak at your event, visit DaciaCoffey.com.

Marketing mix assessment: https://www.themarketingblender.com/assessment/.

Interested in hiring a fractional chief marketing officer or outsourced marketing team? Learn more at themarketingblender.com.

Comments, thoughts, or feedback? Send Dacia a note at dacia@themarketingblender.com.

NOTES

1. *Click*, directed by Frank Coraci (Culver City, CA: Columbia Pictures, 2006).
2. Rick Warren, *The Purpose Driven Life: What on Earth Am I Here For?*, expanded ed. (Grand Rapids, MI: Zondervan, 2012).
3. Sims Wyeth, "Building a Better Mousetrap Isn't Enough—12 Ways You Can Make Your Message Stand Out in a Crowded Marketplace," *Inc*, March 23, 2017, https://www.inc.com/sims-wyeth/build-a-better-mousetrap.html.
4. E. Jerome McCarthy, *Basic Marketing: A Managerial Approach*, 3rd ed. (Homewood, IL: Irwin, 1968).
5. *Merriam-Webster*, s.v. "marketing," accessed August 18, 2021, https://www.merriam-webster.com/dictionary/marketing.
6. American Marketing Association, "Definitions of Marketing," accessed August 19, 2021, https://www.ama.org/the-definition-of-marketing-what-is-marketing/.
7. Barry Popik, "Half the Money Spent on Advertising Is Wasted, but No One Knows Which Half," Big Apple, December 26, 2009, https://www.barrypopik.com/index.php/new_york_city/entry/half_the_money_spent_on_advertising_is_wasted_but_no_one_knows_which_half.
8. Popik, "Half the Money Spent on Advertising Is Wasted, but No One Knows Which Half."
9. CSO Insights, Miller Heiman Group, "All That Glitters Is Not Gold: 2019 World-Class Sales Practices Study," https://www.millerheimangroup.com/resources/resource/all-that-glitters-is-not-gold-results-of-the-2019-world-class-sales-practices-study/.

10 Brent Adamson, Gartner, "CSO Update: The New B2B Buying Journey and Its Implication for Sales," 2019, https://www.gartner.com/en/sales/insights/cso-update.
11 Corporate Executive Board Company, "The Digital Evolution in B2B Marketing," 2012, https://www.thinkwithgoogle.com/future-of-marketing/digital-transformation/the-digital-evolution-in-b2b-marketing/.
12 Accenture, "2014 State of B2B Procurement Study: Uncovering the Shifting Landscape in B2B Commerce," 2014, https://www.accenture.com/t20150624T211502__w__/us-en/_acnmedia/Accenture/Conversion-Assets/DotCom/Documents/Global/PDF/Industries_15/Accenture-B2B-Procurement-Study.pdf.
13 FocusVision, "Content Really Is King: Content Consumption in the B2B Buyer's Journey," 2020, https://www.focusvision.com/resources/content-really-is-king-content-consumption-in-the-b2b-buyers-journey/.
14 CSO Insights, Miller Heiman Group, "2018 Sales Talent Study," https://www.millerheimangroup.com/resources/resource/2018-sales-talent-study/.
15 Aberdeen Group, "The CMO's Agenda: Managing Marketing and Its Alignment with Sales," January 2017, https://channel.report/AberdeenGroup/The%20CMOs%20Agenda%20Managing%20Marketing%20And%20Its%20Alignment%20With%20Sales.pdf.
16 Wheelhouse Advisors, "How to Align Sales & Marketing to Boost Revenue by 208%," February 6, 2015, http://www.wheelhouseadvisors.net/how-to-align-sales-marketing-to-boost-revenue-by-208-infographic/.
17 MarketingProfs, "B2B Content Marketing: 2016 Benchmarks, Budgets, and Trends—North America," 2016, https://contentmarketinginstitute.com/wp-content/uploads/2015/10/2016_B2C_Research_Final.pdf.
18 Marketo, "Top 10 Findings from the Sales and Marketing Alignment Study," accessed August 20, 2021, https://www.marketo.com/webinars/top-10-findings-from-the-sales-and-marketing-alignment-study/.
19 Business Dictionary, s.v. "strategy," accessed May 1, 2020, http://www.businessdictionary.com/definition/strategy.html.
20 US Small Business Administration, Office of Advocacy, "2018 Small Business Profile," 2018, https://www.sba.gov/sites/default/files/advocacy/2018-Small-Business-Profiles-US.pdf.

21 Cintell, "Understanding B2B Buyers: The 2016 Benchmark Study," https://unleashpossibledotblogdotcom.files.wordpress.com/2016/02/final-benchmark-study-understanding-buyers-2016-cintell-2.pdf.
22 Cintell, "Understanding B2B Buyers."
23 HIPB2B, "Infographic—the Science of Building Buyer Personas," April 19, 2019, https://hipb2b.medium.com/infographic-the-science-of-building-buyer-personas-6af0ad1610f9.
24 ITSMA, "ITSMA Online Survey: Increasing Relevance with Buyer Personas and B2I Marketing," May 7, 2014, https://www.itsma.com/research/increasing-relevance-with-buyer-personas-and-b2i-marketing/.
25 Cintell, "Understanding B2B Buyers."
26 ITSMA, "ITSMA Online Survey."
27 ITSMA, "ITSMA Online Survey."
28 Donald Miller, *Building a StoryBrand: Clarify Your Message So Customers Will Listen* (New York: HarperCollins, 2017), 30.
29 Nancy Duarte, "Like Yoda You Must Be," Duarte, accessed August 22, 2021, https://www.duarte.com/presentation-skills-resources/like-yoda-you-must-be-2/.
30 Robert J. Pryor, *Lean Selling: How to Coach Buyers to Make Quicker Buying Decisions and See More Profitable Sales* (Bloomington, IN: AuthorHouse, 2015).
31 Keith M. Eades, *The New Solution Selling: The Revolutionary Sales Process That Is Changing the Way People Sell* (New York: McGraw-Hill, 2004).
32 Eades, *The New Solution Selling*.
33 Chet Holmes, *The Ultimate Sales Machine: Turbocharge Your Business with Relentless Focus on 12 Key Strategies* (New York: Portfolio, 2007), 62.
34 Holmes, *The Ultimate Sales Machine*, 65.
35 Matthew Dixon and Brent Adamson, *The Challenger Sale: Taking Control of the Customer Conversation* (New York: Portfolio, 2011), 72.
36 Ruben Gonzales, *The Courage to Succeed: Success Secrets of an Unlikely Three-time Olympian* (Salt Lake City: Aspen Press, 2004).
37 American Marketing Association, "Definitions of Marketing."
38 American Marketing Association, "Definitions of Marketing."

CPSIA information can be obtained
at www.ICGtesting.com
Printed in the USA
BVHW050034170822
644736BV00001B/66